Moorestown Library

3 2030 00094 9346

NJML Oversized 973.3 Gut
1966.
Guthorn, Peter J.
American maps and map makers of

W9-ALL-128

MOORESTOWN FREE LIBRARY
MOORESTOWN, N. J. 08057

OVERSIZE

973.3   79440
Guthorn, Peter J.
American maps and map makers of
        the Revolution

Moorestown Free Library
Moorestown, New Jersey

AMERICAN MAPS AND MAP MAKERS OF THE REVOLUTION

by Peter J. Guthorn

PHILIP FRENEAU PRESS

MONMOUTH BEACH, N. J.

1966

Copyright 1966
by PETER J. GUTHORN
Library of Congress no. 66-30330

973.3
G

TABLE OF CONTENTS

FOREWORD

The serious student will welcome this important addition to the literature of the American Revolution. It is a unique compilation and fills a serious void.

The book is arranged in orderly fashion. A short biography of each map maker is followed by a list of his known maps. Though frequently fragmentary and based on secondary sources, many of the biographical sketches appear in print here for the first time. A great number of the maps are likewise newly discovered. Each map is briefly described and its repository indicated. The introduction gives additional valuable data.

The author is a prominent New Jersey surgeon who has found time in his busy practice to pursue an unusual avocation. Dr. Guthorn has been a serious student of American maps for many years. Much of the preliminary work on this volume was done at the New York Public Library and led to much interesting discussion between us.

I am happy to see the author's efforts in print.

GERARD L. ALEXANDER
Chief, Map Division
The New York Public Library

1. INTRODUCTION

In a work of this type ready access to highly specialized material is imperative. The writer finds himself both dependent upon and grateful for the cooperation of many individuals and organizations. I could not have asked for more courtesy and assistance than I received as a matter of course from the libraries and staffs of the following institutions: The Boston Athenaeum, the Boston Public Library, the Massachusetts Historical Society, the Harvard University Library, the John Carter Brown Library, the Office of the Secretary of State of Rhode Island, the Newport Preservation Society, the American Antiquarian Society, the Yale University Library, the Connecticut Historical Society, the Connecticut State Library, the New York State Library, the New York Bureau of Surplus Real Property, the Cornell University Library, the New York Historical Society, the New York Public Library, the Pierpont Morgan Library, the Morristown National Historical Park Library, the New Jersey Historical Society, the Princeton University Library, the New Jersey State Library, the American Philosophical Society, the Historical Society of Pennsylvania, Colonial Williamsburg, the Library Company of Philadelphia, the Newberry Library, the William L. Clements Library, the Library of Congress, the National Archives and the Henry E. Huntington Library.

Substantial contributions and suggestions have been made by Mr. Gerard L. Alexander of the New York Public Library, Miss Jeanette D. Black of the John Carter Brown Library, the

79440

late Mr. Arthur B. Carlson of the New York Historical Society, Mr. Howard C. Rice, Jr. of the Princeton University Library, Mr. Samuel S. Smith of the Monmouth County Historical Association, Dr. Walter W. Ristow of the Library of Congress and Mr. Alexander O. Vietor of the Yale University Library. I am indebted to Mr. Paul R. Smith and Mrs. Wilma S. Newhouse for technical advice and to Mr. Daniel I. Hennessey for preparation of the reproductions. The ultimate contribution has been that of my wife Katherine for her encouragement, research, typing and forebearance. The shortcomings of this study are entirely the author's.

There are quite startling and typically national differences between the maps of the Revolutionary War. Those by Americans are extremely varied, reflecting the diverse backgrounds and purposes of their makers. In contrast, those by Europeans tend to be more formalized and similar one to the other, reflecting disciplined training. As a consequence, for proper appreciation of the maps included, a superficial biography of each man precedes a listing of his work.

Contemporary American maps of the Revolutionary War period is the general delineation of this study. The works of European engineers, largely French, who served in the American Army are included. These men had a long standing influence on American military thinking, particularly in the establishment of a national military academy which stressed engineering aspects, and in many other and more subtle ways. A number of these men eventually returned to America as emigrés during the French Revolution. Omitted from this study are the French who served in the expeditionary forces under Rochambeau, D'Estaing and DeGrasse.

The maps themselves are of five major types: military geographical surveys, surveys of encampments and fortifications, casual offhand sketch maps, public information news maps and formal documentary battle maps.

The first, military geographical surveys, were by far the most important from a contemporary view and are of very substantial historical importance. In the days when military movement was earthbound, accurate road maps featuring terrain, bridges, fords and possible sources of forage and food were a necessity. George Washington complained frequently of the lack of adequate maps. The printed maps available were largely English and insufficiently detailed for Army use. In some areas manuscript surveys existed but had been drawn principally to delineate property lines or settle boundary disputes. Furthermore, these were widely scattered, some being in private hands, in the possession of surveyors or occasionally in the offices of Colonial Surveyors-General. Of the latter, duplicates often had been deposited in London and were contributory sources of many printed English Colonial and later military maps. However, even though the colonies were poorly prepared with respect to adequate military maps, they were richly endowed with a few but extremely capable and energetic men to fill the void.

The surveys of fortifications and encampments vary from crude freehand sketches to highly finished renditions. The latter were largely the product of foreign officers in the American Army. These men had an excellent, highly formalized technical background, which, typical of Continental European military philosophy, stressed permanent fortifications and relatively static defenses. The value of these officers, largely French or at least French trained, can not be overemphasized. Not only were they great contributors to the planning of encampments and of static defenses, but they were often fearless and inspired field officers. The foreign engineer officers were a carefully chosen and rigorously trained group. To have detailed knowledge of the chain of fortifications defending a nation's border was to be trusted with secrets of supreme importance almost equivalent to holding key information on today's hydrogen bomb. The military engineer was literate, accurate and trained in the latest scientific developments in ballistics, logistics, mapping, politics, handling of troops and technology in general. It was not until the middle of the eighteenth century that a division of engineering into civil and military was recognized. Prior to that the military engineer was the only one who was formally trained.

The offhand casual sketch maps were, in many instances, shorthand messages representing thousands of words. They were variously employed to show schematically roads, fortifications and troop concentrations. In many cases authorship and even nationality of the map maker is unknown. Many of the maps are so crude that the scale can not be determined; and in a few instances, the exact area is not evident.

The "news story" maps likewise conveyed whole paragraphs with a few sketched lines and brief commentary. Published news was often slow in appearing, frequently heavily biased and inaccurate and giving little idea of the actual events. It was no exception to have a great battle reported by a single correspondent who might very well not have witnessed the battle or who, at best, had seen only a small part of it. Illustrations of battles commonly showed nothing except two opposing files of troops discharging muskets at each other. On the other hand, a map would tell the reader the situation at a glance, even if he were poorly tutored. Some of these were the earliest graphic expressions of the War.

The documentary battle maps were largely in the European tradition. They supplied a current need for graphically recording troop movements, dispositions and features of terrain so that they could be analyzed and studied at a later time. They were also sources of data for condemnation or praise of the commanding officers. There is a very human tendency to remember victories and forget defeats. The English and Continentals with their professionalism viewed the results of battle in a somewhat more detached way than did the Americans who demonstrated the amateur's and volunteer's partisanship.

Most of the maps in this study fall into one of the five main categories although a few fall into more than one. As previously noted, the training, background, ability and productivity of the map makers varied immensely, their very diversity being an American Colonial characteristic. Training ranged from nil to extensive formal education as surveyor, draftsman or trained mathematical cartographer. Productivity ranged from one to hundreds. Each map maker identified herein is accorded a biographical sketch to the extent that pertinent information is available, largely from secondary sources. In no sense has a definitive biography been attempted even where it would have been possible. In a few cases, where the individual is well known historically, notably in the case of George Washington, a detailed outline has been omitted entirely. However, most of the men were of secondary importance historically. This does not detract from their contributions as map makers but relates to their influence in initiating or commanding historical events. They were not commonly authors of or recipients of voluminous correspondence, signers of important documents or parties to important conferences or meetings. Rather, most are known by virtue of their map or maps and from a very few contemporary references.

The total accomplishments of our group of map makers, however, were of great contemporary and historical importance. Unfortunately they have been assimilated into the total picture and have gone virtually unnoticed as an entity, not being newsworthy by ordinary standards. It is hoped that with recognition of their great contribution will come discovery of further maps by many of these men.

It has seemed necessary to include men who were not map makers in the strict sense but who were printers, publishers and engravers. Their inclusion makes this study more panoramic but the contributions were so important as to warrant it.

It is noteworthy that a number of the men were members of the American Philosophical Society of Philadelphia, which was organized in 1769 and served as a National Academy of Science. It is also of interest that a large number of these men were acquainted with one another and knew one another's work.

This study is a personal survey founded on years of interest and has been organized as a descriptive and presumably preliminary check list. I anticipate that further suggestions and indications of omissions by readers may enable completion of the list and correction of possible errors. All the maps are contemporary or are surviving copies of contemporary originals which have disappeared. Eclectic maps have been omitted entirely as have retrospective maps unless made immediately after the event. Excluded also have been the contributions of several Loyalists and American officers who eventually became Loyalist, notably Benedict Arnold, Daniel Hammill, Nathaniel Hubbill, John Lawrence and Thomas Millidge, among others. Maps on exotic materials or in unusual media are beyond the scope of this study.

A notable future contributor who is omitted because he made no known maps during the period of study is Thomas Hutchins. Hutchins was born in Monmouth County, N. J. in 1730, spent his youth on the Pennsylvania frontier and served in the Colonial troops in 1757 during the French and Indian War. He then entered the British service but resigned in 1780 because unwilling to bear arms against his fellow countrymen. During his British service he received engineering training so that he was able to lay out Fort Pitt and the fortifications at Pensacola. He published "A Topographical Description of Virginia, Pennsylvania, Maryland and North Carolina" in London in 1778 and "An Historical, Narrative and Topographical Description of Louisiana and West Florida" in Philadelphia in 1784. He was elected a member of the American Philosophical Society in 1771.

Hutchins' Revolutionary War service started in May 4, 1781 with his appointment as Geographer to the Southern Army under General Greene. On July 11, he was appointed Geographer to the United States but produced no surveys or maps because of illness. His outstanding contribution came in perfecting the system for plotting western territory public lands for government sale under the ordinance of May 20, 1785.

Selection of material has been easy in the case of printed maps. Date and origin are usually evident and authorship is generally known.

Manuscript maps present problems if the authorship and date are not definitely indicated. The repository, watermarks, history if available, notes on accession, language, descriptive terms, type of survey and handwriting may provide clues. Many of the western expeditions are a case in point. An author may be presumed to be English or at least Loyalist in sympathy when the language of the map is English, allusion is made to "rebels" or "rebel forces" and "indication of American position with the garrison for reducing it" or " where the 40th Regiment entered" is noted. To complicate matters, some Hessian and French map makers labeled some of their maps correctly in English.

Manuscript maps in French could have been made by French officers serving in the American Forces, by French officers serving under Rochambeau or DeGrasse or finally, by some of the Hessians who had trained in France or who affected French as a distinction. Many French maps are unsigned; and there are occasionally more than one manuscript map of the identical engagement or geographical region which are nearly but not quite the same. The attribution in this group has been made on the basis of the best current information but again is open to at least some question.

Another confusing factor arises as the result of the technical and military dominance of French arms and science in the 17th and 18th centuries. French ideals, idiom, language and ideas permeated and dominated the trained corps of officers and scientists of most of Europe. It was distinctive for Continental and other military officers to have been educated in their science in France. This was equivalent to the German domination of similar fields in the late 19th and early 20th centuries.

Certain areas received a large share of interest from map makers, for example, the Highlands of the Hudson River, the Boston area, the New York Bay area, the Delaware River below Philadelphia and the Yorktown area. These were the sites of obvious conflict or were of great importance in communications. They were also areas which were heavily fortified, were the scene of numerous engagements and were coincidentally areas in which many foreign trained officers served. Other areas received little attention. There are few maps of the western campaigns with the exception of those of the expeditions of Colonel William Butler and General John Sullivan against the Indians of Western New York.

The illustrative examples have been selected on the basis of cartographic interest, relative importance and representation of as many map makers and types of maps as possible. Some which would have been included on the basis of these criteria have been omitted because of difficulty in reproducing them adequately. In order to do justice to all the maps of the Revolution, separate volumes should be allotted to the English and their allies, the French Expeditionary Forces and to those other and anonymous map makers including the many spies who do not fit into these categories.

The map makers have been arranged alphabetically for no better reason than convenience. Following a short biographical sketch, the particular man's maps are given individually by title and location. Features of interest are noted on a highly selective and subjective basis. Measurements are given in inches, to the inside of borders on maps so supplied, and of the overall size of maps without borders. When a map is unique or rare, the repository has been indicated.

Initially a discussion of contemporary surveying methods, description of instruments and methods of map plotting and construction had been planned. However, it has been omitted as a comprehensive section is to be included in the forthcoming revised edition of Silvio A. Bedini's "Early American Instruments".

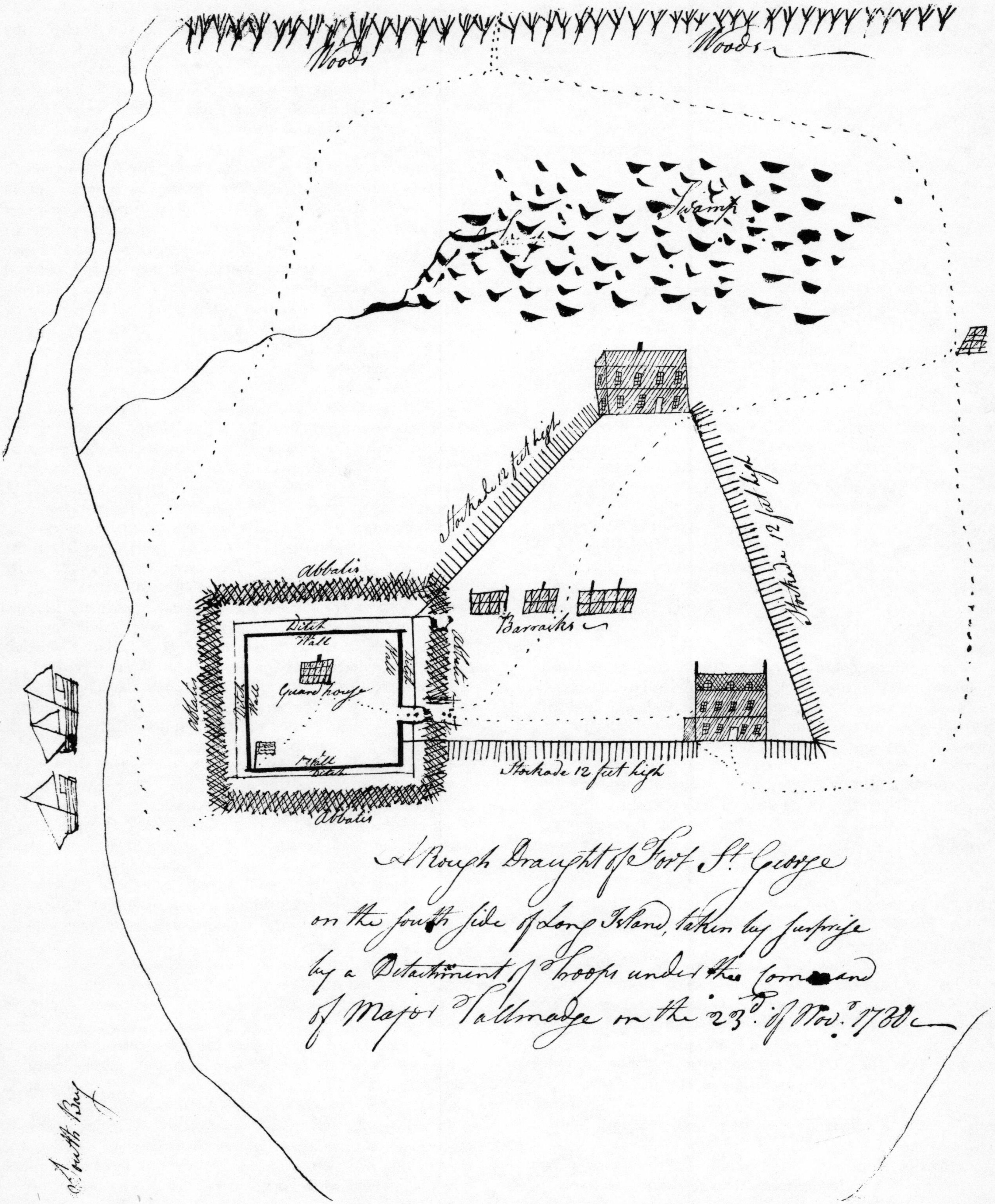

Woods

Woods

Swamp

Abbatis

Ditch
Wall

Wall

Abbatis

Wall

Guard house

Wall
Ditch

Abbatis

Barracks

Stockade 12 feet high

Stockade 12 feet high

Stockade 12 feet high

A Rough Draught of Fort St. George on the south side of Long Island, taken by surprise by a Detachment of Troops under the Command of Major Tallmadge on the 23d. of Nov.o 1780

South Bay

Fort St. George, Long Island, captured by Major Benjamin Tallmadge. Connecticut Historical Society.

2. ROBERT AITKEN

Robert Aitken was born in Dalkeith, Scotland, in 1734. After serving an apprenticeship in the book trade, he came to Philadelphia as a bookseller in 1769. He found things to his liking, returned to England and brought his family back to Philadelphia in 1771. During the next years he worked as an engraver, bookbinder, bookseller, publisher and editor.

Aitken was the pioneer publisher of a tradesman's account book in 1773. From January 1775 to June 1776 he published *The Pennsylvania Magazine or American Monthly Museum.* This organ was edited by Thomas Paine and represented the partisan views of the publisher. It contained a number of maps of interest.

Aitken is best known for publication of the New Testament and the first complete Bible in English in America. He was a bookbinder of outstanding ability. Incidentally, he was a witness to the will and codicil of map maker Robert Erskine. Aitken died in Philadelphia in 1802. The following maps are to be found in the Library of Congress, the New York Historical Society and others.

(1) A NEW MAP OF NORTH & SOUTH CAROLINA & GEORGIA.
Copper engraving 7⅜ x 8¾.
June 1775. *Pennsylvania Magazine.*

(2) A NEW AND CORRECT PLAN OF THE TOWN OF BOSTON AND PROVINCIAL CAMP.
Copper engraving 7⅜ x 10¼.
July 1775. *Pennsylvania Magazine.*
This is very much like a map published in the *Gentlemen's Magazine,* London, January 1775.

(3) EXACT PLAN OF GENERAL GAGE'S LINES ON BOSTON NECK IN AMERICA.
Copper engraving 8¾ x 11½.
August 1775. *Pennsylvania Magazine.*

(4) A CORRECT VIEW OF THE LATE BATTLE AT CHARLESTOWN, JUNE 17, 1775.
Copper engraving.
September 1775. *Pennsylvania Magazine.*

(5) A MAP OF THE PRESENT SEAT OF WAR ON THE BORDERS OF CANADA.
Copper engraving 6 x 15⅛.
October 1775. *Pennsylvania Magazine.*

(6) PLAN OF THE TOWN & FORTIFICATIONS OF MONTREAL, OR VILLE MARIE IN CANADA.
Copper engraving 6½ x 9¼.
November 1775. *Pennsylvania Magazine.*

(7) A PLAN OF QUEBEC, METROPOLIS OF CANADA IN NORTH AMERICA.
Copper engraving 4¼ x 7.
December 1775. *Pennsylvania Magazine.*

(8) TO HIS EXCELLENCY, EDWD. CORNWALLIS ESQ.; GOVERNOUR & C. OF HIS MAJESTY'S PROVINCE OF NOVA SCOTIA IN AMERICA & C. THIS MAP OF THE PROVINCE OF NOVA SCOTIA AND PARTS ADJACENT, IS HUMBLY PRESENTED BY HIS EXCELLENCY'S MOST OBEDIENT AND DEVOTED HUMBLE SERVANT JAMES TURNER.

Copper engraving 13¼ x 17¾.
"Printed and Sold by R. Aitken in Philadelphia 2 edition 1776". This map has inset plans of "The Situation of Halifax Drought of the Harbour & c.", "Plan of Halifax", "Plan of Quebec", "City & Port of Louisbourg" and "View of Boston" in perspective. It was advertised on the back cover of the *Pennsylvania Magazine* for December 1775. "This day is published and to be sold by R. Aitken Bookseller, opposite the London Coffee-House. Printed on a Large Sheet of Demy Paper (price two-shillings)". "A Correct Map of the Great River St. Lawrence, Nova Scotia, New-Foundland, and that part of New England, in which may be seen the March of Col. Arnold, from Casco Bay to Quebec, by the way of Kennebec River, ornamented with small Plans of Quebec, the Town of Halifax and its Harbour, and a small Perspective View of the City of Boston". It was a republication of Turner's map which had been made in Philadelphia in 1759 for the French and Indian War. The Turner imprint has been scratched out and the date altered. Aitken's promotion of this old map which had suddenly become timely is obvious.
Turner had engraved Lewis Evans' map of 1755, Joshua Fisher's Chart of Delaware Bay in 1756, and the map in the New Jersey Bill in Chancery in 1747. Library of Congress.

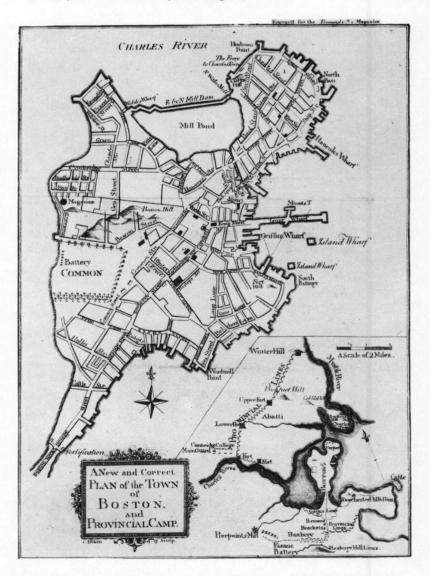

ROBERT AITKEN. *"Boston and the American Camp"* published in his *"Pennsylvania Magazine"* for July 1775. New York Historical Society.

3. EDWARD ANTILL

Edward Antill was born at Piscataway, New Jersey, on April 11, 1742. He graduated from King's College (now Columbia College) in 1762 with an AM degree, and was admitted to the practice of law in New York, but subsequently moved to Quebec. He became a member of the American Philosophical Society in 1768. When Quebec was besieged by the Americans under Arnold in 1775, Antill was permitted to join them. He was assigned as Chief Engineer by General Richard Montgomery. When the assault on Quebec by Montgomery and Arnold failed, Antill was sent by General David Wooster to take the news of Montgomery's death and failure to General Schuyler and the Continental Congress. Antill at this time held the rank of Lieutenant Colonel in Hazen's 2nd Canadian Regiment. He made his map of Quebec following the death of Montgomery on December 31, 1775 since the location of the barrier where Montgomery fell is identified.

In May 1776 Antill was assigned as Adjutant General of the American Army in Canada under Arnold. In December of the same year he was sent on a recruiting tour through New Jersey and the southern states. His success earned a letter of commendation from Washington and $2,000 in expenses as voted by the Congress.

Antill was captured by the British on Staten Island August 22, 1777 while under the command of Sullivan. By pure chance, his brother who was in the British service found him and obtained his parole. He was not exchanged until November 2, 1780 and was retired finally from service January 1, 1783.

Antill started law practice in New York but gave it up to return to Canada in 1785. Subsequently he was appointed Judge of the Court of Common Pleas in Clinton County, New York. However, he died at St. Johns, near Montreal, on May 21, 1789 before being sworn in.

(1) GENL. ARNOLD'S PLAN OF QUEBEC WITH THE AMERICANS BESIEGING IT WINTER 1776.
In lower right corner "E. Antill lt". A carefully drawn, detailed manuscript survey with many points of great historical interest. 15 x 18½. In the Sparks Collection, Cornell University.

4. J. ARMSTRONG

J. Armstrong was probably John Armstrong, born in New Jersey on April 20, 1755 and later a resident of Pennsylvania. During the Revolution, Armstrong served in the 12th and 3rd Pennsylvania Regiments with the rank of Captain. Following the War, he served under General Harmar on the frontier and contributed other maps. Armstrong died February 4, 1816.

Armstrong's maps were made in the fall of 1780 in the Morristown, New Jersey area and were drawn for Erskine. As usual, Erskine gave credit to the surveyor.

ERSKINE-DEWITT MAP 118. FROM MORRISTOWN TOWARDS SUSSEX C. H. BY J. ARMSTRONG, A. B. & C.
A. FROM MORRISTOWN TO SUCCASUNNY. Manuscript survey. 12¼ x 15.
B. FROM SUCCASUNNY TO MUSCONETEUNK ON THE ROAD TO SUSSEX. Manuscript survey. 12½ x 15.
C. ROAD FROM MORRISTOWN TO SUSSEX CONTINUED TO AMOS PETITS. Manuscript survey. 12¼ x 14¾.
   New York Historical Society.

5. SEBASTIAN BAUMAN

Sebastian Bauman was born at Frankfurt-am-Main, Germany in 1739, was educated at Heidelberg and served as an engineer in the Austrian service. He emigrated to New York in time to serve in the French and Indian Wars.

Bauman's Revolutionary War service started with his appointment as Captain of a New York Militia Company known as "the German Fusiliers." On March 30, 1776, he was appointed Captain of a New York Artillery Company. He was transferred to the 2nd Continental Artillery January 1, 1777 and was promoted to Major September 12, 1778. Bauman was assigned as Artillery Commander at West Point in 1779 and while there he met Chastellux and was present at Arnold's defection. In 1781 he was third in command of Lamb's Artillery which was ordered to Yorktown. Here he was one of the officers in command of the besieging batteries, the greatest concentration of artillery in any engagement during the Revolution.

Bauman must have begun his study of the battleground soon after Cornwallis' defeat because a prospectus for his planned map was published in the *New-Jersey Journal,* January 30, 1782. The undated rough manuscript in the American Philosophical Society was probably by Bauman. The map was engraved by Robert Scot of Philadelphia. A letter from Bauman to Baron Steuben dated June 26, 1782 indicates that the map was then being printed. Steuben had placed an order for 40 copies.

Bauman was discharged from service January 17, 1783 and was appointed first Federal Postmaster of New York City, a position he held until his death October 19, 1803.

(1) PLAN OF YORKTOWN IN VIRGINIA.
Three manuscripts presented to the American Philosophical Society, October 7, 1831 by Richard Randolph. These are not signed but were identified at the time of donation. #1 is a rough sketch in pencil and color with extensive descriptive notes and is 17½ x 22½ inches. #2 and #3 are rough pencil sketches which fit together, respectively 17¼ x 12 and 17¼ x 12½ inches.

(2) TO HIS EXCELLENCY GENL. GEORGE WASHINGTON COMMANDER IN CHIEF OF THE ARMIES OF THE UNITED STATES OF AMERICA THIS PLAN OF THE INVESTMENT OF YORK AND GLOUCESTER HAS BEEN SURVEYED AND LAID DOWN, AND IS MOST HUMBLY DEDICATED BY HIS EXCELLENCY'S OBEDIENT AND VERY HUMBLE SERVANT, SEBASTIAN BAUMAN M'OR OF THE NEW YORK OR 2ND REGT OF ARTILLERY.
This notation appears on the upper right hand corner. In the upper left hand corner is a detailed reference to the armaments, etc., of the British lines. In the lower center, surrounded by a highly ornamental cartouche of flags and military accoutrements, is a detailed description of the allied forces. At the top of this is the note: "This Plan was taken between the 22nd & 28th of October 1781". Across the bottom "Note, the land within the dotted lines has been laid down by surveys". "R. Scot Sculp Philad 1782". Ships, both afloat and sunken are shown in the York River. The detailed description of artillery, rather than of the military forces, indicates Bauman's background. The attractive and handsome engraving is 19 x 25½ inches.

(3) TO HIS E(XCELLENCY) G(ENERAL) WASHINGTON COMMANDER IN CHIEF OF THE ARMIES OF THE UNITED STATES OF AMERICA THIS PLAN OF THE INVESTMENT OF YORK AND GOUCESTER (SIC) HAS BEEN SURVEYED AND LAID DOWN AND IS MOST HUMBLY DEDICATED BY HIS EXCELLENCY'S OBEDIENT AND VERY HUMBLE SERVANT, SEBASTIAN BAUMAN, MAJOR OF THE NEW YORK OR 2ND REGI-

MENT OF ART. WALDSCHMIDT 1782.
This manuscript copy of Bauman's printed map is in the Library of
Fort Monroe, Virginia.
(4) TO HIS E(XCELLENCY) G(ENERAL) WASHINGTON,
COMMANDER IN CHIEF OF THE ARMIES OF THE UNITED
STATES OF AMERICA THIS PLAN OF THE INVESTMENT OF
YORK AND GOUCESTER (SIC) HAS BEEN SURVEYED AND
LAID DOWN, AND IS MOST HUMBLY DEDICATED BY HIS EX-
CELLENCY'S OBEDIENT AND VERY HUMBLE SERVANT (SIC)
SEBASTN. BAUMAN MAJOR OF THE NEW YORK OR 2ND
REGIMENT OF ART.
A finished, colored manuscript copy of Bauman's printed map is
signed at the bottom "Waldschmidt 1785". The references are iden-
tical. Size is 17½ x 18¾ inches. The William L. Clements Library.

6. HENRY BAWBEE

Henry Bawbee was a Wyandot Indian Chief. The Wyan-
dots, a Huron tribe, were firm allies of the British.
NEW FORT AT DETROIT.
A highly schematic but detailed and carefully labeled sketch map.
10½ x 13¼. At top "B Henry Bawbee his riting". Enclosed in a
letter from General Daniel Brodhead at Fort Pitt to General Washington at New Windsor, December 7, 1780. Library of Congress.
Washington Manuscripts.

7. JAMES BOWDOIN

James Bowdoin was born in Boston on September 22, 1752.
He was the only son of Governor James Bowdoin, a wealthy
merchant. Young James graduated from Harvard in 1771 and
then went on to further studies at Oxford. Although an ardent
patriot, ill health prevented participation in the armed forces.
James subsequently became a successful merchant; and in
November 1805, was appointed United States Minister to
Spain. Unfortunately, the rapid military and political changes
in Europe prevented his assumption of the position. Bowdoin,
like other American representatives, was unable to cope with
Napoleon's diplomacy and returned to farm his estate on
Nashuan Island in Buzzard's Bay. Bowdoin died on October
11, 1811 and left his fortune, property and fine collection of
drawings and paintings to Bowdoin College.
PLAN OF HALIFAX HARBOUR.
Careful manuscript copy of Le Rouge's map of 1778, 9¼ x 11½. Scale
of miles at bottom, labeling in English. Soundings are indicated. The
original French descriptive title is given with an explanatory note
following. The map was enclosed in a letter from Bowdoin in Boston
to General Washington at Morristown, May 31, 1780. Library of
Congress. Washington Manuscripts.

8. FERDINAND DE BRAHM

Ferdinand Joseph Sebastian de Brahm was in the service of
the Prince-Elector of Treves prior to coming to America in
1776. He was commissioned Major of Engineers in the Continental forces on February 11, 1778.
After serving in the north, de Brahm was taken prisoner at
Charleston in May 1780. His journal of the siege at Charleston
was later published by Gibbs in his *Documentary History*.
De Brahm was exchanged on April 24, 1781, was promoted to
Lieutenant Colonel on February 6, 1784 and subsequently retired from service. He was a member of the American Philo-

sophical Society.
(1) THE NEW YORK CAMPAIGN OF 1776.
A detailed sketch map, with references, of the Long Island and Fort
Washington campaigns. 12¾ x 16. William L. Clements Library.
(2) THE NEW YORK CAMPAIGN OF 1776. 1777.
A finished colored manuscript map, with references as above. 13¹/₁₆
x 16½. William L. Clements Library.
(3) PLAN OF THE TOWN OF PURISBURG & THE CAMP OF
JUNE 1, 1779.
A finished manuscript wash drawing 9½ x 12 without border. New
York Public Library.

9. JACOB BROOM

Jacob Broom was born in Wilmington, Delaware in 1752.
He was the son of a blacksmith. He attended Wilmington's Old
Academy and later trained as a surveyor. His cartographic con-
tribution was a regional map made in 1777 and used by Washington in the Brandywine campaign. Broom served in many
posts, including those of Burgess, Representative to the Federal
Convention, State Legislative Representative and Postmaster of
Wilmington. He died in Philadelphia in 1810 and was interred
in Christ Churchyard near Franklin's grave.
(BRANDYWINE CAMPAIGN)
"Laid down at 200 p^S in an inch, the 27th day of August, An. Dom.
1777, pr Jacob Broom, surv^R, N. Castle." This large scale manuscript
is 59 by 19 inches, with two additional sections of irregular shape 10
by 16 and 15½ by 18 inches. The map extends from Bohemia and
Elk River on the south to Kennett Square north of the Brandywine.
It is dated two days after General Howe and the British Army landed
at the head of the Elk River on their march to Philadelphia. There is
excellent road and stream detail and there are also numerous notes in
the hand of George Washington. Historical Society of Pennsylvania.

10. JOHN CADWALADER

John Cadwalader was born in Philadelphia in January 1742.
He was the son of a doctor. Educated at the College and
Academy of Philadelphia (now the University of Pennsylvania), he entered business and soon accumulated a substantial
fortune. He was a member of the American Philosophical
Society.
Cadwalader was a member of the Philadelphia Committee
of Safety and an ardent patriot. He became successively Captain
of the Philadelphia City Troop, Colonel of the Philadelphia
Battalion and Brigadier General of the Pennsylvania Militia;
he took part in the Battles of Princeton, Brandywine and Germantown. His cartographic contribution was made on the eve
of the Battle of Princeton.
Cadwalader was a strong supporter of Washington against
the so-called "Conway Cabel" and engaged in a duel with
Conway in which the latter was wounded. Cadwalader died in
Shrewsbury, Maryland in 1786.
(PRINCETON AND VICINITY)
A crude manuscript draft 9¾ x 15¾ inches. Made by Cadwalader
from information furnished by a spy and sent to Washington December 31, 1776 from Crosswicks. The Library of Congress.

11. MICHEL CAPITAINE DU CHESNOY

Michel Capitaine du Chesnoy was born in Mezieres in 1746.
After training as a geographical engineer, he became a Lieutenant in the Regiment of Aquitaine in November 1770. He

came to America as one of Lafayette's three aides and was commissioned a Captain in the Corps of Engineers in April 1778. In this post, his principal function was to record in maps the engagements in which Lafayette took part.

Capitaine was promoted to Major in 1778. He returned to France temporarily with Lafayette until March 1780. He returned to France for the last time after the Yorktown campaign and died in November 1804.

(1) A New Plan of Boston Harbor From An Actual Survey (by Capitaine) 1776.
Reproduced in the Karpinski Collection (157) from the original in the French War Office.

(2) Carte de L'Action de Gloucester Entre un Parti Americaine D'Environs 250 Hommes Sous le g^L Lafayette et un Parti des Troupes de Lord Cornwallis Commande par le g^{EL} Apre Son Sorties Dans le Jersey le 25 9bre 1777.
Carefully drawn ms. colored 16 x 20 inches. In Sparks Collection, Cornell University (MSI 539).

(3) Plan de la Retraite de Barrenhill en Pensilvanie on un Detachment De Deux Mil Deux Cent Hommes sous le Gal Lafayette etait entourné par L'Armee Anglaise Sous le Genx Howe, Clinton, et Grant le 28 May 1778.
Carefully drawn ms. 14¼ x 19½ inches. A table of references contains items A through R which are nearly identical with those on maps 4, 5, 6 and 7. In addition there is item S, "point de la rivière on les sauvages la passe pour rejoindre la detachment". In addition "Chestnut Hill" is labeled on this but not on maps 4 and 5, although its location is indicated. Incidentally, the engagement took place on May 20. Yale University Library.

(4) Plan de la Retraite de Barrenhill en Pensilvanie on Un Detachment de 2,200 Hommes Sous le General la Fayette, etait entourné par L'Armee Anglaise Sous le G^{EN} Howe, Clinton et Grant le 28 Mai 1778.
Carefully executed ms. measuring without border, 13 x 20¼. "Major Capitaine A.D.C. du gl Lafayette" in lower left. Reference A-R. Historical Society of Pennsylvania (Am. 602).

(5) Plan de la Retraite de Barrenhill en Pensilvanie on un Detachment de 2,200 Hommes Sous le General la Fayette, etait entourné par L'Armée Anglaise Sous les Généraux Howe, Clinton, et Grant

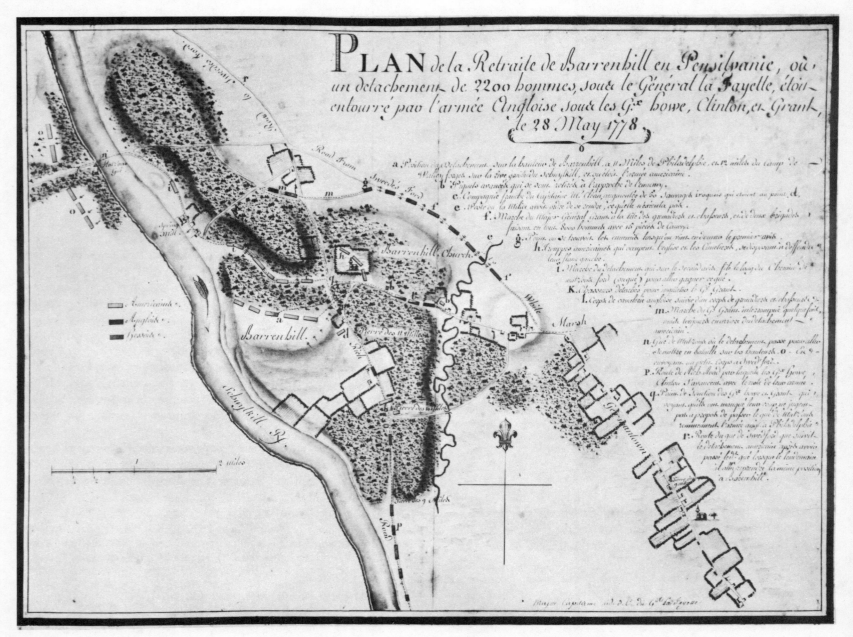

Michel Capitaine du Chesnoy. "The Retreat at Barrenhill". One of five nearly identical manuscript maps. Capitaine was an aide to Lafayette and was responsible for documenting his engagements in maps. John Carter Brown Library.

LE 28 MAI 1778.
Careful colored ms. 13½ x 18½ in border. This was copied from the original in the possession of Lafayette, under his supervision for Jared Sparks. Reference A-R.
Sparks Collection, Cornell University Library (MPI 538.)

(6) PLAN DE LA RETRAITE DE BARRENHILL EN PENSILVANIE ON UN DETACHEMENT DE 2,200 HOMMES SOUS LE GENERAL LA FAYETTE, ETAIT ENTOURNÉ PAR L'ARMEE ANGLAISE SOUS LES GX HOWE, CLINTON ET GRANT LE 28 MAY 1778.
Colorful manuscript 14 x 19 within borders. References A-R.
John Carter Brown Library.

(7) PLAN DE LA RETRAITE DE BARRENHILL EN PENSILVANIE OU UN DETACHMENT DE DEUX MILLES DEUX CENS HOMMES SOUS LE GENERAL LA FAYETTE ÉTAIT ENTOURRÉ PAR L'ARMÉE ANGLAISE SOUS LES GEN[AUX] HOWE, CLINTON ET GRANT LE 28 MAY 1778.
Reproduced in the Karpinski Collection (178) from the original in the "archives des cartes ministere de la guerre."

(8) CARTE DE L'AFFAIRE DE MONMOUTH ON LE GÉNÉRAL WASHINGTON COMMANDAIT L'ARMÉE AMERICAINE, ET LE GÉNÉRAL CLINTON COMMANDAIT L'ARMÉE ANGLAISE LE 28 JUIN 1778.
Carefully drawn ms. 14¼ x 28½. The title is on the upper left and the "Légende" contains 24 references. Sparks Collection. Cornell University. (MPI541a.)

(9) CARTE DE L'AFFAIRE DE MONTMOUTH ON LE GENERAL WASHINGTON COMMANDAIT L'ARMEE AMERICAINE ET LE GEN[AL] CLINTON L'ARMÉE ANGLAISE LE 28 JUIN 1778.
Carefully drawn ms. with a "Légende" containing 24 references to the battle. The title is across the top above the border. French Ministry of War, reproduced in the George Washington Atlas as plate 40 and included in Karpinski Collection as number 183.

(10) PLAN DE LA BATAILLE DE MONTMOUTH ON LE G[L] WASHINGTON COMMANDAIT L'ARMÉE AMERICAINE ET LE G[L] CLINTON L'ARMÉE ANGLAISE, LE 28 JUIN 1778.
Copperplate engraving 8½ x 15¼ inches published in M. Hilliard D'Auberteuil "Essais Historiques sur la Révolution De l'Amerique Septentrionale" Brussels and Paris 1782. The explanatory note contains 22 references which correspond closely with those of maps 8/9.

(11) CARTE DES POSITIONS OCCUPÉES PAR LES TROUPPES AMERICAINES APRÉS LEUR RETRAIT DE RHODE-ISLANDE LE 30 AOUST 1778.

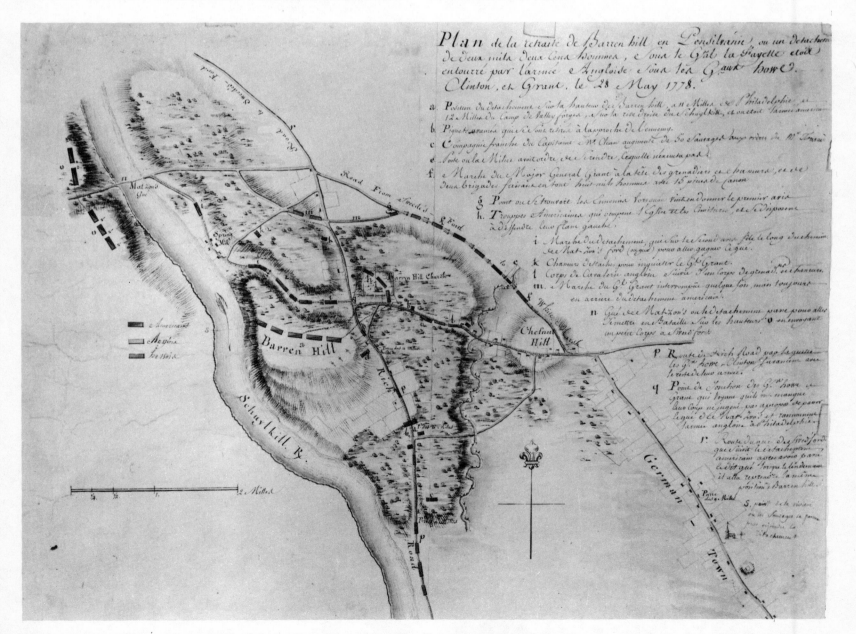

MICHEL CAPITAINE DU CHESNOY. *An unsigned copy of "The Retreat at Barrenhill". It is nearly identical to the others but contains one additional reference to the site of the crossing of "les sauvages", a small detachment of indians. Yale University Library.*

Carefully drawn, colored ms. 12 x 20¼ inches with border. In lower right "Major Capitaine A.D.C. du G¹ LaFayette". Preservation Society of Newport County. Newport, Rhode Island.

(12) CARTE DE POSITIONS OCCUPÉES PAR LES TROUPES AMERICAINES APRES LEUR RETRAITE DE RHODE-ISLAND LE 30 AOUT 1778.
Carefully drawn ms. 12½ x 18¾ inches, colored with border. Sparks Collection. Cornell University. (MPI 543).

(13) PLAN DE RHODE-ISLAND AVEC LES DIFFERENTES OPERATIONS DE LA FLOTTE FRANCAISE ET DES TROUPES AMERICAINES COMMANDÉE PAR LE MAJOR GENERAL SULLIVAN, CONTRA LES FORCES DE TERRE ET DE MER DES ANGLAISE, DEPUIS LE 9 AOUT, JUSQU'A LA NUIT DU 30 OU 31 DE MÊME MOIS 1778 QUI LES AMERICAINES ON FAIT LEUR RETRAITE.
Carefully drawn ms. 12¼ x 30 inches. Contains a great number of references including the location of Bishop Berkeley's residence. Berkeley was the revered philosopher and clergyman who had resided in Newport for only three years starting in 1748. Sparks Collection. Cornell University. (MPI 542).

(14) CARTE DU THÉATRE DE LA GUERRE EN AMERIQUE SEPTENTRION^LLE PENDANT LES ANÉES 1775, 76, 77 ET 1778.
Capitaine du Chesnoy, Cap^NE d'Inf^RIE Photostat 13¾ x 17¾ in the Library of Congress (360187-27) from original in the French Hydrographic Service. The size of the original is not known. The map covers the East coast from Cape Ann to the Upper Chesapeake. Gives a great deal of detailed information on engagements. Fort Arnold at West Point is shown. The same map is reproduced in the Karpinski Collection as number 467.

(15) CARTE DU THEATRE DE LA GUERRE DANS L'AMERIQUE SEPTENTRIONALE PENDANT LES ANNÉES 1775, 76, 77 ET 78 OU SE TROUVENT LES PRINCIPEAUX CAMPS AVEC LES DIFFERENTE PLACES ET EPOQUES DES BATAILLES QUI SE SONT DONNES PENDANT CES COMPAGNES . . . FAIT PAR SR. CAPITAINE DU CHESNOY.
Printed map 25½ x 29 "Chez Perrier Graveur . . . ã Paris" A_____ _____ from an atlas and numbered on verso No. 54. In collection of Mr. John F. Reed, King of Prussia, Pa.

(16) PLAN OF THE HARBOUR AND CITY OF ANNAPOLIS 1781 DONE BY MAJOR CAPITAINE AID OF GENERAL LAFAYETTE.
Karpinski Collection. (177) Original in the French War Office.

(17) CARTE DE LA CAMPAGNE EN VIRGINIE DU MAJOR GÉNÉRAL M^IS DE LA FAYETTE OU SE TROUVENT LES CAMPS ET LES MARCHES AINSI QUE CEUX DE LIEUTENANT GENERAL L^D CORNWALLIS PAR LE MAJOR CAPITAINE AID DU CAMP DU G^EL LA FAYETTE EN 1781.
Finely drawn colored ms. 35 x 44. Colonial Williamsburg.

(18) CARTE DE LA CAMPAGNE EN VIRGINIE DU MAJOR GÉNÉRAL M^IS DE LA FAYETTE OU SE TROUVENT LES CAMPS ET LES MARCHES AINSI QUE CEUX DE LIEUTENANT GÉNERAL LORD CORNWALLIS EN 1781.
Carefully executed, colored ms. 36½ x 58½. Yale University Library.

(19) CARTE D'UNE PARTIE DE LA PROVINCE DE NEW YORK ET DES JERSEYS.
A colorful ms. within border from Raritan Bay on the south to Haverstraw on the north, including Long Island, New York Island and adjacent New Jersey. 47.2 x 63.2 cm. Reproduced as number 141 in the Karpinski Collection.

It was noted before that Capitaine's principal function was to make maps of the engagements in which Lafayette took part. Capitaine's illnesses may have accounted for a few of the inconsistencies. According to Jared Sparks, quoted in the Catalog of his Library, maps numbered in this study as 2, 5, 8, 12 and 13 were manuscript copies made for Mr. Sparks during his visit to France where the originals were in the possession of Lafayette. The copies themselves were made under Lafayette's direct supervision. Although none of these handsomely executed copies on handmade paper bear Capitaine's name, his authorship is a reasonable assumption. The precise history of the originals bearing Capitaine's name are unknown but map 10 may have been made from number 9 which was in Lafayette's possession at that time. Map makers frequently made more than a single copy but rarely indicated this fact. The copies often varied in size, finish and detail. Map number 11 was finally included as probably copied from an original by Capitaine although there are some doubts.

12. JOHN CLARK, JR.

John Clark, Jr. of Lancaster, Pennsylvania, was appointed a 1st Lieutenant in the 2nd Battalion of Miles Pennsylvania Rifle Regiment, March 15, 1776. On January 14, 1777, he became an Aide to General Nathaniel Greene. The accompanying map was made shortly thereafter.

Clark was promoted to Captain in the Pennsylvania State Regiment February 20, 1777 and later was transferred through other Pennsylvania units. Clark was discharged on June 3, 1783 and died December 27, 1819.

A MAP OF THE RARITAN RIVER & ADJACENT COUNTRY WITH A PLAN OF THE ROADS.
Title on verso. A schematic but carefully executed map covering an area bounded by Perth Amboy, Griggs Town, Worleys Tavern and White's Tavern. 14½ x 19. There is a scale of miles, two miles to an inch and "Note, This sketch of the River Raritan was laid down by a scale of two miles to an inch the general course of the River from the forks to Amboy is supposed due East the meeting of the River from the forks to Amboy is supposed due East the meeting of the Road are incorrect but from Brunswick to the fork near the Mouth. The dotted lines from White's Tavern to Millstone Court House is the rout of the Enemy's Light Horse when they took Maj. General Lee near Baskingridge. To the Hon^BLE Major General Greene this map is presented by his obed^T friend Jno. Clark, jun. Morristown Feby 11th 1777." Princeton University Library.

13. J. DENISON

J. Denison is not definitely identified but is most likely Joseph Denison II of Stonington, Connecticut, who owned a large farm in South Kingston, Rhode Island. Joseph Denison II died in 1785 in Stonington and left a large family. Another Joseph Denison of Stonington was born in 1708 and died in 1795; while John Denison was Stonington Town Clerk during the same period. Several of the maps in the 1796 edition of Morse's "The American Universal Geography" are by a J. Denison, presumably the same man. One of these is also included in the 1802 edition of the same book.

(1) (NARRAGANSETT BAY AND RHODE ISLAND)
An accurate, careful but unsophisticated manuscript plan of the military and naval operations between August 10 and 30, 1778. It is within a border, with a scale of miles at bottom. "J. Denison Scripsit". 15¼ x 18½. Massachusetts Historical Society.

(2) (NARRAGANSETT BAY AND RHODE ISLAND)
An accurate, careful but unsophisticated manuscript plan of the military and naval operations between August 10 and 30, 1778, within borders and colored. Scale of miles at bottom. "J. Denison Scripsit". Rhode Island Secretary of State.

14. Simeon DeWitt

Simeon DeWitt was born in Ulster County, New York, on December 25, 1756. He was the son of Dr. Andrew DeWitt and attended Queen's College, now Rutgers, from which he graduated as the sole member of the class of 1776. His courses included the natural and mental philosophy of mathematics and logic.

DeWitt entered the Continental Army as a private and participated in the Saratoga Campaign. His uncle, General James Clinton, recommended him in 1778 as an assistant to Robert Erskine, newly appointed Geographer to the Continental Army. DeWitt immediately began work in this capacity and succeeded to the post as Geographer-in-Chief following Erskine's death December 4, 1780. He apparently proved to be the one among Erskine's many assistants capable of carrying out the Department's mission. Prior to Erskine's death, DeWitt's name is attached to maps 66 and 106. All the remainder of the maps through 131 were completed under DeWitt's direction. No-

table are the surveys of the roads to Williamsburg and Yorktown in Virginia which were finished in time for use by Washington's Army en route and return from victory.

After the surrender at Yorktown in October 1781, DeWitt continued his work as Geographer with headquarters in Philadelphia. Apparently no further surveys were completed but some finished maps were probably prepared from the rough field sketches at hand. In 1783 DeWitt proposed that the military road maps be used in publishing a map of the state of war in America but was turned down because of expense. In 1784 he again proposed using the military surveys. This matter was considered but died for want of support. On May 13 of the same year, DeWitt resigned his post to become Surveyor-General of the State of New York, which post he held until his death on December 3, 1834. He was a member of the American Philosophical Society.

DeWitt retained many of the field surveys made by him and by Erskine but these were never used. They were finally

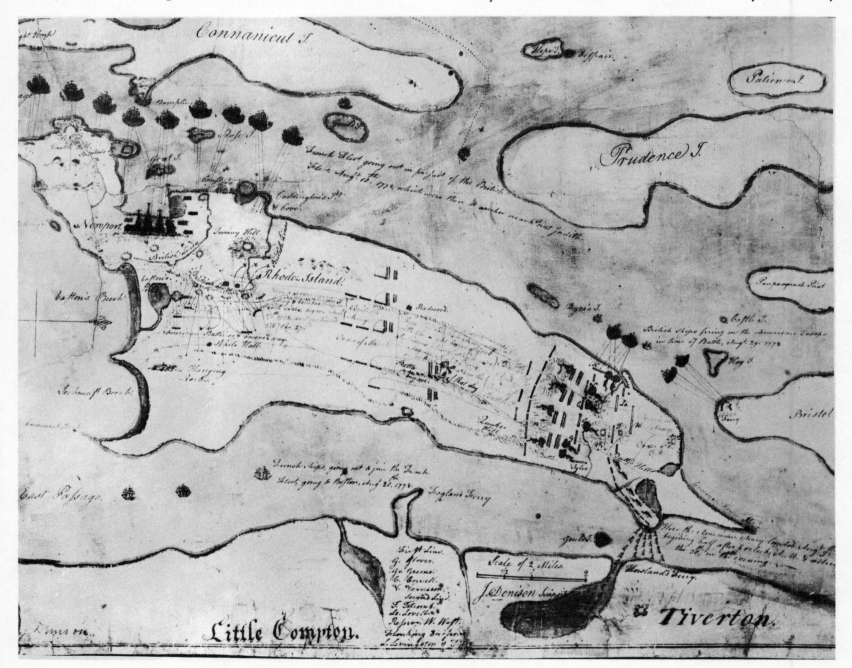

J. Denison. *Part of the map of the Rhode Island operations of August 1778. Massachusetts Historical*

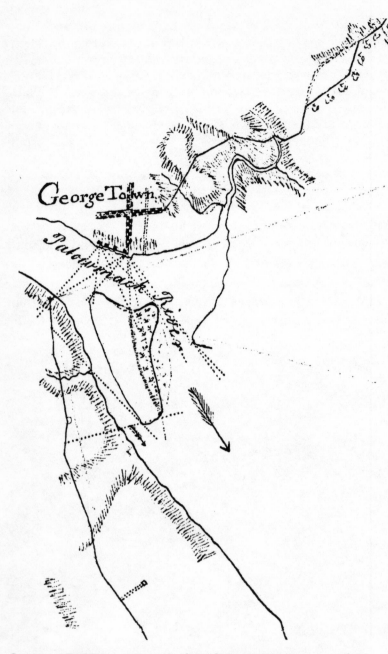

SIMEON DEWITT. *Detail of Erskine-DeWitt map 124 "from Bladensburgh to near Alexandria through Georgetown". New York Historical Society.*

presented to the New York Historical Society by DeWitt's grandson, Richard Varick DeWitt, in 1845.

The employment of the Erskine-DeWitt surveys as partial source material for Christopher Colles' survey of the roads of the United States has been studied extensively by Dr. Walter W. Ristow of the Library of Congress. Most of the Erskine-DeWitt maps are roughly finished plane-table sketches of the roads and immediately adjacent features such as taverns, habitations, fords, swamps and commanding elevations. Usually the surveys were made on a scale of one mile to the inch. Labeling was cursive; and most maps had the title and number enclosed in a diamond shaped, quadrilateral or oval outline cartouche. Contractions on a larger scale were made with more attention to the niceties of lettering, shading and finish. A few highly finished surveys were made.

The following maps have been numbered in accordance with the original list of rough drafts of surveys started by Robert Erskine in 1778. All are in the New York Historical Society

with a few exceptions which are noted. Most are rough drafts, primarily of roads, unless otherwise noted.

(66) NEW YORK, PHILAD^A & NEIGHBORING COUNTRY—8 MILES TO AN INCH.
Partially finished ms. of New Jersey north of latitude 39° 50′ including eastern Pennsylvania, Western Long Island, the present Westchester County etc. Titles are partially cursive and partially printed. Size is 14 x 17½ inches with a finished border with latitude and longitude indicated, the prime meridian passing close to Tappan, New York. The map is projected on a conic grid and is similar to that made by Erskine for George Washington's use. The southern borders are identical but the prime meridian differs.

(106A) CONTRACTION IN THE JERSEYS. 1 MILE AN INCH.
A partially finished map partly in cursive and partly printed on a conic projection. It covers an area roughly bounded by present-day Perth Amboy, Passaic, Morristown and Somerville. Size is 21¼ x 29 inches.

(106B) CONTRACTION IN THE JERSEYS. 1 MILE AN INCH.
Similar to the above. 19½ x 29½ inches in size. Directly contiguous and south of 106A.

(115) COUNTRY BETWEEN HUDSON & DELAWARE.

(116) BETWEEN PASSAIC & PARAMUS, HACKENSACK & ZABRISKIE'S 1780.
13 x 16 inches.

(117) FROM MT. PLEASANT TO NEW GERMANTOWN, & FROM PLUCKEMIN TO BLACK RIVER. 1780, A. B. C.
A. *From Near Squire Fullers thro Succasunny to Flanders.* 12¼ x 14¼.
B. *From Flanders to Horton.* 12¼ x 15¼.
C. *From Pluckemin to Black River.* 12½ x 15.

(119) FROM SUSSEX C. H. TO PITTSTOWN & RINGOES AND BACK PAST THE UNION, & FROM HACKETTSTOWN TO N. GERMANTOWN. A, B, C, D, E, F.
A. *From Sussex Court House to New Hackettstown.* 18¼ x 23¼.
B. *From Hackettstown to Johnson Upper Mills.* 19 x 25½.
C. *From Johnsons Upper Mills to Pittstown & Ringoes.* 19 x 23½.
D. *From Near Ringoes' tow^D the Union.* 19 x 23¾.
E. *Past the Union to Lewis's Tavern.* 19 x 23½.
F. *From Hackettstown to New Germantown.* 19 x 23¾.

(120) NEAR THE WHITE PLAINS ACROSS FROM SAW MILL RIVER TOWARDS THE BRUNKS TO NEAR THOS. THOMPSONS.
4¼ x 5¼ (this is glued on map #59).

(121) FROM WHERE A ROAD BRANCHES OFF TO MIDDLE BUSH TO TRENTON. A, B.
A. *To Princeton & a little way further.* 19 x 21¾.
B. *From Princeton to Trenton.* 19 x 23.

(122) THE ENVIRONS OF KINGSBRIDGE.
17¾ x 18¾.

(124) THE ROUTE TO YORK IN VIRGI. A, B, C, D, E, F, G, H, I, K, L, M, N, O, P, Q, R, S, T, U.
A. *From Philadelphia through Derby & Chester to the Anchor Tavern.* 18 x 18¼.
B. *From the Anchor Tavern through Wilmington & Newport & past Christiana Bridge & across Couches Bridge over the south end of Iron Hill to a little past the division line into Delaware.* 19 x 24.
C. *From the head of Elk to the Brick Meet'g House.* (small inset "N.B. this from Scull's Survey".) 19 x 24.
D. *From Head of Elk to near Susquehanna.* 19¼ x 23¾.
E. *From Susquehanna to Bushtown.* 19 x 23¾.
F. *From near Bushtown & Newtown to Past Nottingham Iron Works.* 19 x 23¾.
G. *From near Nottingham Iron Works to Baltimore.* 19 x 24.
H. *From Baltimore past Elkridge till past Rowling's Tavern.* 19 x 24.
I. (missing).
K. *From near Governor's Bridge to near Bladensburgh.* 19 x 24.
L. *From Bladensburgh to near Alexandria past Georgetown.* 19 x 24.
M. *From Alexandria to near Colchester.* 19 x 24.
N. *From Colchester past Dumfries to Stafford Court House.* 19 x 24.
O. *From Stafford Ct. House past Falmouth, Fredericksburgh & Todds*

Ordinary to the Mattepoyne thence down the same to Near the Bowling Green Ordinary. 19 x 24.

P. From the Bowling Green Ordinary past the Red House across the Mattaponye past Burke's Ordinary to near Head Lynche's Ordinary. 19 x 23¾.

Q. From Head Lynche's Ordinary across the Pamunky River to some distance past Hanover Court House. 19 x 23¾.

R. From near Hanover Court House through Hanover & New Castle Towns to near Johnson's Tubmill on Meredecun. 19 x 23¾.

S. From Johnson's Tubmill past New Kent Ct. Ho. to Thomas Rauson's Ordinary. 19 x 24.

T. From near Rauson's Ordinary past Duncastle alias Bird's Ordinary to near Allen's Ordinary. 19 x 23¾.

U. From Allen's Ordinary through Williamsburgh to York. 19 x 23¾.

(125) THE ROUTE FROM VIRGINIA. A, B, C, D, E, F, G, H, I, K.

A. (The Route back from Virginia) Beginning on the road from Williamsburgh to Hanover one mile 54 chains & 20 links from Duncastle towards Hanover, thence across the Pamunky at Ruffin's Ferry to a Brick Church. 18¼ x 24.

B. (Back from Virginia) From near to Brick past King William Ct. Ho. and the Burnt Ordinary to near Aylett Mills. 19¼ x 23¾.

C. From Aylett's Mill past Aylett's Warehouse across Todd's Bridge and Moroscosick. 19 x 23½. Second piece 10¾ x 14 attached.

D. From John Hampton's on the road from Todd's Bridge to the Red House (see sheet C) past Gardiner's Ordinary, Beverly's Mill and Sneed's Ordinary & across the Rappahannock River to Port Royal Tavern. 19 x 23¾.

E. From near Port Royal to Hooes Ferry on the Potomac River. 19 x 23¾.

F. From Hooes Ferry to Port Tobacco. 18¾ x 23¾.

G. From near Port Tobacco to Piscataway. 19 x 23½.

H. From Piscataway toward Bladensburgh. 19 x 24.

I. Past Bladensburgh. 19 x 23¾.

K. Past Snowden's Iron Works to Elkridge Landing. 19¼ x 20¼.

(126) CAMP AT VERPLANK'S POINT 1780. (missing).
2nd. not labeled or finished.

(127) THE LINE BETWEEN PENNSYLVANIA & MARYLAND.
16½ x 24. Detailed, highly finished survey with long descriptive "Explanation" at bottom. From Rittenhouse's survey(?)

(128) ROADS FROM NEW WINDSOR TO GOSHEN, FLORIDA, CHESTER &C.
18½ x 24½.
2nd. Roads from New Windsor to Goshen, Florida, Chester &c. 20 x 25¾.
3rd. Same. 14¼ x 14½.
4th. From Coldenham towards Goshen and Walkill Road. 11¼ x 16¾.

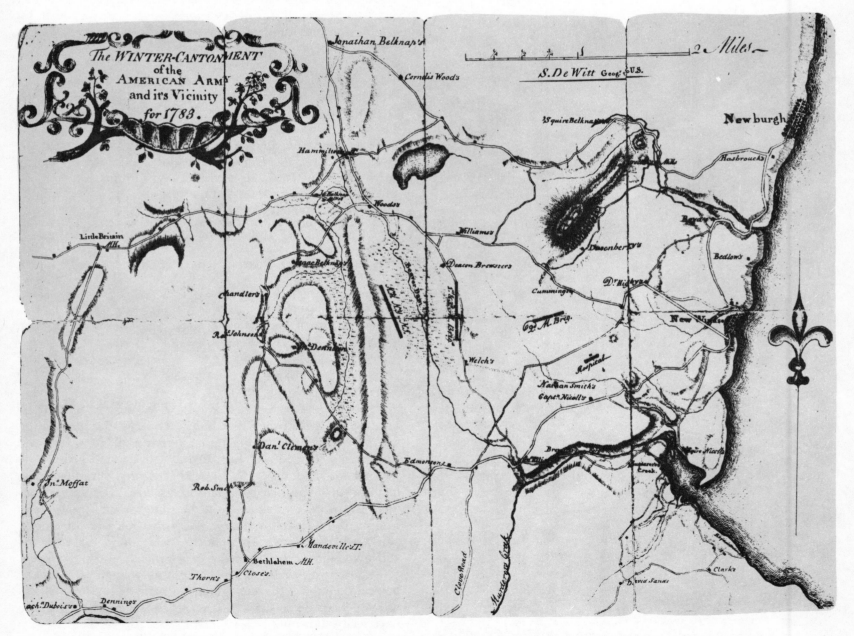

SIMEON DEWITT. The last cantonment of the Continental Army, at New Windsor. New York Historical Society.

15

5th. No title. 15 x 21½. This may be a topographical survey of the Palisades.

(129) MOORE'S LAND AT W. POINT. (missing).

(130) NO TITLE.
Survey composed of many small sheets to make up a sheet 16 x 30¼. The location is not indicated but shows "Hay's Tavern", "Gills Ford", "Andrew's Ford", "Road to Guthries's Ford suvd by Capt. Gray", "Road to Motherells Tavern".
2nd. *Road from Little Britan's Meetg Ho. to Peach Bottom Ferry.* On bottom is "Lancaster Road". 11 x 14¼.

(131) NO TITLE.
20 x 29¾. Fishkill River, Peekskill Hollow, Mohopack Pond etc. plotted on a grid.

THE WINTER CANTONMENT OF THE AMERICAN ARMY AND ITS VICINITY FOR 1783.
10½ x 14½ carefully drawn map with title in ornamental cartouche. Details of encampment by regiment, showing hospital, roads and local residents.

ROBERT ERSKINE. *Portion of Erskine-DeWitt map 93 between Albany and Kinderhook. New York Historical Society.*

VERPLANKS' POINT.
Detailed survey 11¼ x 11¾ showing Kings Ferry, troop disposition, roads and residents. In lower right "S. DeWitt Geog^R — Sept. 19th 1782". Sparks Manuscripts, Harvard University Library. (PF158).

15. LOUIS DUPORTAIL

Louis LeBeque de Presle Duportail, the son of a lawyer, was born in 1743 at Pithiviens near Orléans, France. He attended military school at Mezieres and graduated as an officer of engineers in 1761.

Duportail came to America in 1777 in the company of two other engineers, LaRadiere and Gouvion, and was commissioned a Colonel of Engineers on July 8th of that year. He was promoted to Brigadier General November 17, 1777. He was employed in the defense of Philadelphia, laying out Fort Mifflin and later, the defenses of Valley Forge. As a result of his proven ability, Duportail was made Commandant of the Corps of Engineers and Sappers May 11, 1779. He contributed to the design of the fortifications at West Point, principally by compressing its spread out plan.

Duportail was taken prisoner at Charlestown May 12, 1780 but was exchanged in time to attend the important Weathersfield Connecticut Conference in May 1781 and later the Dobbs Ferry Conference. He was promoted to Major General November 16, 1781 and was retired October 10, 1783.

Duportail returned to France where he, as did many other French officers who served in America, played a part in the French Revolution. He became Minister of War in 1790; but, due to a shift in the political situation, returned to America in 1794 where he lived quietly on a farm near Valley Forge. An invitation to return to France and glory prompted his setting sail for home in 1802. He died at sea on this final voyage.

(1) "PLAN DU CAMP DE VALLIE FORGE".
A detailed but unfinished ms. 11¼ x 15¼ showing the encampment and the earlier fortifications. This was probably prepared in December 1777 and may be the initial map of Valley Forge. Historical Society of Pennsylvania.

(2) PLAN OF THE POSITION OF VALLEY FORGE, 7TH JAN. 1778.
Manuscript map 9¼ x 14¾, title on verso. Library of Congress.

(3) (PAULUS HOOK).
Manuscript map of fortifications at Paulus Hook in descriptive letter. 6¾ x 7¼. Library of Congress.

16. PIERRE-EUGENE DuSIMITIERE

Pierre-Eugene DuSimitiere was born in Geneva, Switzerland in 1736, arrived in the West Indies about 1750 and made his way to Philadelphia in 1776 after tarrying in New York and Burlington. In Philadelphia he was active as an artist, antiquarian and naturalist. His "cabinet of natural curiosities" was quite possibly the first collection of its type. His natural history "Museum" was situated on the north side of Arch Street below 5th. Chastellux visited the collection and dubbed it paltry and noted that DuSimitiere "was still a bachelor and still a foreigner", both worthy of comment.

DuSimitiere was one of Philadelphia's early portraiturists and helped to establish the iconography of many famous Americans of the period. He was also a voracious collector of books. These were sold following his death and form a part of the collection of the Library Company of Philadelphia. Some are in the

Library of Congress. He was a member of the American Philosophical Society.

DuSimitiere's one cartographic contribution was made for Aitken, a fellow member of the American Philosophical Society. DuSimitiere died in 1784 and was buried in St. Peter's Churchyard, Philadelphia.

MAP OF THE MARITIME PARTS OF VIRGINIA EXHIBITING THE SEAT OF WAR AND OF LD. DUNMORE'S DEPREDATIONS IN THAT COLONY.

Copper engraving with border. 9¾ x 10¾ in the *Pennsylvania Magazine,* April 1775, p. 184.

17. ROBERT ERSKINE

Robert Erskine, the son and grandson of Presbyterian clergymen, was born in Dunfermline, Scotland, in 1735. He attended the nearby University of Edinburgh in 1747, 1748 and 1752 but did not graduate. The next 19 years were spent mainly in London. During that time he went into partnership in the hardware business which ended in financial embarrassment.

Erskine evinced interest in a variety of scientific fields. His papers in the New Jersey Historical Society contain excellent wash drawings of instruments, including a quadrant with artificial horizon, a complicated "Platometer" consisting of circles and arcs which may have been designed to solve spherical trigonometric problems graphically, a sextant and other instruments of sophisticated design. A description of the "Platometer" describes its use "to find the latitude & variation of the needle at sea any time of the day by two observations of the sun". Other manuscripts are "on the longitude", the effects of bridges and abutments as a cause of shoals and a centrifugal pump. There is also a survey of a stream system and one letter addressed to him as "Mr. Robert Erskine, Land Surveyor and Engineer, next to the Crown, Scotland Yard, London". These were obviously busy years spent in highly technical accomplishment. The character of Erskine is evident from his careful writing of his theses, meticulous corrections, interlining and rewriting. One exercise sums up his character, the message being "application with industry", "application joind (sic) with industry". His application and industry were rewarded with Fellowship in the Royal Society on January 31, 1771. Sir John Pringle proposed him and Benjamin Franklin seconded him. The next man to be admitted to Fellowship was Alexander Dalrymple, another Scot and pioneer British Admiralty hydrographer of the South Seas.

Erskine had made a tour and inspection of some of the English iron mills and furnaces from early September 1770 to the end of October in preparation for his migration to America to head the American Iron Works. He arrived in New York on June 5, 1771 and immediately became immersed in the problems of operation of the iron works at Ringwood, Long Pond, Charlotteburg and adjacent properties in the highlands of Northern New Jersey. His record books, correspondence and public notices indicate his energy and organization. It was during these years that he first made the acquaintance of William Alexander, Lord Stirling, Surveyor-General of New Jersey, iron mine proprietor and later Revolutionary War general.

The Revolution found Erskine representing the interest of the English stockholders but loyal to the Colonial cause. He outfitted and drilled a company of employees as militia, probably with the aim of keeping his labor force and protecting the properties.

It was not long before the need for accurate surveys became evident to Washington and the potential abilities of Erskine recognized, apparently because he had supplied a map to General Charles Lee in December 1776. Thus began Erskine's outstanding work.

The first map Erskine supplied, which is in the Morgan Library in New York, is "A Map of part of the States of New-York and New-Jersey, laid down chiefly from actual surveys received from the Right Honorable Lord Stirling and others and Delineated for use of his Excellency General Washington by Robert Erskine FRS 1777." The map includes all of New Jersey north of Gloucester, the adjacent parts of Pennsylvania and New York. There are numerous notations in Washington's hand. The map was folded to pocket size and saw hard service.

William Alexander, the self-styled Lord Stirling, had served in the French and Indian War and had been appointed Surveyor-General of New Jersey in 1756, succeeding his father James. He had rendered aid to Lewis Evans and to Thomas Pownall in making their respective maps of the Middle British Colonies in 1755 and 1775. Alexander owned an estate at Basking Ridge, New Jersey and had interests in North Jersey iron mines through which he probably made Erskine's acquaintance. Prior to Erskine's arrival in America, Alexander had been one of a group rendering a detailed report on the properties of the American Iron Works to Governor Franklin of New Jersey in 1772. Alexander was captured during the Battle of Long Island, exchanged and later attained the rank of Major General.

On July 27, 1777 Erskine was appointed Geographer to Washington's army. His accomplishments are largely covered in one of his letters: "From Surveys actually made, we have furnished His Excellency with maps of both sides of the North (Hudson) River, extending from New Windsor and Fishkill, southerly to New York; eastward, to Hartford, Whitehaven, etc., and on the west to Easton in Pennsylvania. Our Surveys likewise include the principal parts of New Jersey, lying northward of a line from Sandy Hook to Philadelphia; take in a considerable part of Pennsylvania; extend through the whole route of the Western army under Gen'l Sullivan; . . . on both sides of the River, to Albany & from thence to Scoharie. In short, from the Surveys made, and materials collecting and already procured, I could form a pretty accurate Map of the four states of Pennsylvania, New Jersey, New York and Connecticut . . .". "In the spring of 1777 I began to do business for the Public, by making a sketch of the Country for Gen'l Lee; a map of the Jerseys for His Excellency Genl. Washington from material furnished by Lord Stirling . . .". By February 12, 1780, the surveys had required altogether "upwards of two hundred and fifty sheets of paper." This was a tremendous accomplishment for a small group of men in little more than two and a half years.

Examination of the manuscript surveys themselves demonstrate that though most are rough field sketches, they are accurate, detailed, show features of terrain and are on the large scale of a mile to the inch. These route surveys were subsequently incorporated into smaller scale contractions with a scale varying from 2 to 8 miles to the inch. These were plotted on a grid of conic projection in which the prime meridian was New York City. The greater number of the manuscripts are in the New York Historical Society. The collection also has a manuscript list of the rough drafts in Erskine's hand. The last notation is Number 114 "Contraction of D° & Sundry places Rectified". Erskine contracted pneumonia and died October 2, 1780, the same day Major John Andre was executed. Simeon De-Witt succeeded to Erskine's post. He was a member of the American Philosophical Society.

In addition to DeWitt, others played a greater or lesser part in building this great collection of surveys. These were David Pye, William Gray, William Scull, John Watkins, Benjamin Lodge and J. Armstrong. When their contribution is of sufficient importance and where biographical material has been obtainable, they have been accorded individual mention. It is evident that on occasion Erskine could be not only critical but caustic. He accorded Lodge a dressing down directly on Map 79A.

Erskine and DeWitt used the data and surveys of others, for example the map of New York and New Jersey already cited as being from surveys furnished by William Alexander, Lord Stirling; Map 40, the course of the Farmington River from bearings taken by a Mr. Porter in 1765; Map 88, Albany County by a Mr. Vromer (probably Vrooman) and Map 89, the Schuylkill River by David Rittenhouse. The latter may also have been the source of Map 127, the line between Pennsylvania and Maryland. Credit was always given to the original surveyors.

The somewhat haphazard choice of geographical area to be surveyed represents the orders of Washington anticipating the probable course of hostilities. This in itself is worthy of study and consideration.

Most of the maps listed are plane table road surveys, commonly on a scale of one mile to the inch. The exceptions as to location of the map, type or scale are noted. Erskine's own numerical designations have been employed. The titles and lettering are in cursive, the titles and numbers being surrounded by a rectangular, diamond shaped or round cartouche. The titles used here are taken from "A List of the Rough Draughts of Surveys by Robert Erskine, F.R.S. Geogr. AUS and Assistants begun A.D. 1778" and also from the titles of the individual maps themselves, when the information is complementary. Therefore some maps may have both collective and individual titles. Among the conspicuous inconsistencies are the varied spellings of proper names and capitalizations.

A MAP OF PART OF THE STATES OF NEW-YORK AND NEW-JERSEY, LAID DOWN CHIEFLY FROM ACTUAL SURVEYS RECEIVED FROM THE RIGHT HON^BLE L^D STIRLING & OTHERS AND DELINEATED FOR THE USE OF HIS EXCELLENCY GEN^L WASHINGTON BY ROB^T ERSKINE FRS 1777.
A carefully drawn ms. with border showing degrees and division. The prime meridian passes through New York City. There is a scale of miles and chains at the bottom. The entire map is 24½ x 38½, is drawn on four sheets of paper which are badly weathered and stained, and is projected on a rectangular grid. This was used by Washington as a pocket map and bears numerous notations in his hand. Much of the map appears to have been copied from contemporary printed English maps, probably Samuel Holland's. Pierpont Morgan Library.

A. (NEW YORK CITY, NORTHERN NEW JERSEY, WESTCHESTER COUNTY AND THE HUDSON RIVER AS FAR AS NEW WINDSOR).
"Sketch by R. Erskine FRS, Geographer to the Army of the United States 1778." A partially finished ms. 15 x 18¼.

B. Part 1 (NORTH EASTERN NEW JERSEY, THE HUDSON HIGHLANDS, WESTCHESTER COUNTY, WESTERN CONNECTICUT, WESTERN LONG ISLAND AND NEW YORK BAY TO THE BASE OF SANDY HOOK).

Carefully drawn partially finished ms. within borders. 17½ x 24.
C. (HUDSON HIGHLANDS AND ADJACENT AREA).
"Capt. Gray (started at) the 75 milestone and proceeded up the Clove to New Windsor & New Bourough cross at Con(tinental) Ferry & survey to Fishkill from whence to Peekskill & Kings Ferry when he shall and Mr. Lodge to begin at the 15 milestone and proceed by Suffrans to Kings Ferry then cross and proceed to Tarry Town. Mr. Henderson to begin at Kings Ferry and proceed through the mountains at Dunderberg off Montgomery thence to fort Arnold thence to Murders Creek and End after his mark the Road at Renow (?) Dock." Crude ms. in pencil and ink on both sides of a sheet. 13¼ x 16¾.

D. NEW WINDSOR.
Careful detailed pencil and ink sketch of the town. 14 x 15¾.

E. SKETCH OF THE COUNTRY ABOUT NEW WINDSOR.
And the roads intersecting it with names of the principal inhabitants. Finished pen and ink. 14 ¾ x 21¾.

F. MENSURATION ON THE ICE FEB. 7TH 1780.
Rough ink sketch of the Hudson River from latitude 41° approximately 20 miles north. 13¼ x 17.

A MAP OF THE EAST SIDE OF THE NORTH RIVER DONE IN CONSEQUENCE OF ORDERS FROM HIS EXCELLENCY GEN^L WASHINGTON.
Carefully drawn, finished manuscript map 15½ x 36. Scale of miles at bottom. "Scale 2 miles to an inch". Notation "N.B. all roads with double lines an actual survey". The area covered by the map is rough bounded by Paulus Hook, Newburgh, New Fairfield, Stamford and New York City. Although authorship is not indicated, it is undoubtedly by Erskine. New York Public Library.

A MAP OF THE HIGHLANDS IN THE STATE OF NEW YORK DONE FOR HIS EXCELLENCY GENL WASHINGTON BY ROBERT ERSKINE F.R.S. GEOG. TO THE ARMY JULY 1779.
Carefully executed ms. extending from the New York-New Jersey Border to north of Newburgh 15 x 8¾. Scale, 2 miles to an inch. The map has been folded and has seen hard use. Historical Society of Pennsylvania (Am 6213).

The following were made during 1778
unless otherwise indicated.

(1) ROAD FROM SUFFERANS TO JUNE'S, KING'S FERRY FORT MONTGOMERY &C. (VERSO) PEEKSKILL, TELLER'S POINT, TARRYTOWN &C.
A. Part 1. 19 x 28½.
Part 2. 13½ x 25¾.
B. Part 1. (missing)
Part 2. *Vicinity of Fort Montgomery.* 13¾ x 20.
C. (missing)
D. *Nichol's Hill, North R^R, Butter Hill &c.* 13¼ x 20. Dec. 1777.
E. *Contraction of a Road from Cortlandt Furnace towards Crum pond.* 1 mile to an inch. 8½ x 13¼.

(2) ROAD FROM FT. MONTGOMERY TO WEST POINT &C. (missing)

(3) ROAD FROM D^O TO FORREST OF DEAN &C.
8¼ x 14¼.

(4) ROAD FROM JUNE'S UP THE CLOVE. (missing)

(5) CONTINUATION OF ROAD THROUGH THE CLOVE, TO NEW BOROUGH.
13¼ x 15¾.

(6) ROAD FROM NEW BOROUGH TO PEEKSKILL.
15 x 19.

(7) ROAD FROM NEW BOROUGH TO PEEKSKILL.
On opposite side of No. 6.

(8) ROADS FROM PEEKSKILL TO WHITE PLAINS, MAMARONECK &C. &C..
Sheets joined. (missing).

(9) ROAD FROM WHITE PLAINS TO DOBB'S FERRY.
12¼ x 17¾.

(10) D^O FROM D^O TO EAST CHESTER. (missing)

(11) TUCKEHO ROAD.
10 x 16¼.
(12) ROAD FROM TARRYTOWN TO CROTON RIVER.
11¾ x 20.
(13) SAWMILL RIVER ROAD, VALENTINE'S HILL, POST ROAD.
16¼ x 22½.
(14) ROAD FROM HARMON'S TO GEN'L GATES, WHITE PLAINS. (missing)
(15) ROAD FROM ARTILLERY PARK W. PLAINS TO DOBBS FERRY, RD. D°. (missing)
(16) CROSS ROAD ABOVE DOBB'S FERRY FROM POST RD. TO SAW-MILL RD.
11 x 12¼.
(17) ROAD BETWEEN SAWMILL & TUCKEHO, N&S. (missing).
(18) ROAD FROM YOUNG'S TAVERN TO WHITE PLAINS.
12¼ x 16.
(19) CROSS ROADS TO EAST CHESTER AND ABOVE.
15 x 19.
(20) ROAD FROM THE WHITE PLAINS TO BLOOMERS MILL AT RYE NECK AND CROSS ROADS.
14¼ x 19½.
(21) FROM WHITE PLAINS TO KING'S STREET, FROM KING STREET TO WRIGHT'S MILL.
11 x 12.
(22) FROM ANDREW PURDY'S TOWARDS DAVENPORTS AND FROM JOSEPH CARPENTER'S TOWARDS SING SING.
12½ x 13.
(23) FROM CROTON BRIDGE TOWARDS THE N. RIVER AND FROM MICHL LOUNSBURY'S TO DAVENPORT'S TAVERN.
13 x 16¾.
(24) FROM SAW-PITTS TO STANWICK, STAMFORD, BEDFORD & PINE BRIDGE ON CROTON RIVER.
20½ x 24¼.
2nd. & From Stanwich to King Street.
20¼ x 24¼.
(25) A CONTRACTION OF DITTO (joined to 59).
(missing)
(26) See under *Watkins*.
(27) See under *Pye*.
(28) FROM BEDFORD TO RIDGEFIELD, DANBURY &C.
3 sheets. (missing).
(29) FROM FISHKILL TO FREDERICKSBURG, CROTTON BRIDGE, QUAKER HILL &C.
5 sheets. (missing).
(30) FROM PINE BRIDGE OR CROTTON TOWARDS FREDERICKSBURG & CROSS TO PEEKSKILL.
4 sheets. (missing)
(31) ROADS FROM BEDFORD TO DANBURY.
12¾ x 17½.
(32) ROADS FROM PEEKSKILL TO PINES BRIDGE ON CROTON RIVER &C.
14 x 18½.
(33) ROAD FROM STAMFORD TO GREENWICH. (missing)
(34) A CONTRACTION OF D°. (missing)
(35) DRAUGHT OF THE ROADS FROM FISHKILL TO DANBURY &C &C.
21 x 33½.
(36) ROADS FROM NEWBOROUGH TO FORT LEE.
15¼ x 32¾.
part 2- 17¼ x 25.
part 3- 17¼ x 24½.
(37) A GENERAL CONTRACTION.
2 miles to an inch. On many small sheets joined to form two sheets

18 x 26 and 20½ x 26½ of irregular shape. Detailed, partially finished survey of the Hudson River from New York City, through the Highlands to Newburgh with roads, towns and terrain for twenty miles inland on each shore. Plotted on carefully constructed grid. The third sheet is missing.
(38) ROAD FROM JUDGE JAY'S NEAR FISHKILL TO ROBINSONS MILLS.
13 x 27.
(39) ROAD FROM NEW MILFORD TO HARTFORD & BACK TO BULL'S IRON WORKS. (missing)
(40) See under *Porter*.
(41) ROAD FROM RINGWOOD TO SLOTT'S ON THE NEW WINDSOR ROAD.
12½ x 20.
(42) ROADS FROM RINGWOOD TO POMPTON PLAINS AND FROM POMPTON PLAINS TO SUFFRANS.
21 x 22.
(43A) FROM WOODBURY TO THE CONTINENTAL BRIDGE NEAR NEWTOWN.
13¼ x 15¾.
B. *Through Newtown.* 12¾ x 13.
C. *Through Danbury to Southbury.* 8 x 16¼.
D. *From Southbury to Croton.* 9½ x 17½.
E. *From Theles Tav. to Crumpond & towards Robinson's Stores.* 9 x 16½.
(44) CONTRACTION OF THE ROADS FROM DANBURY TO CRUMPOND.
5 x 14½.
(45) CONTRACTION OF THE ROADS FROM BELOW ROBINSON'S MILLS TO PEEKSKILL.
8¼ x 12.
(46) 1st. ROADS FROM POMPTON TOWARDS MORRISTOWN.
13½ x 16¾.
2nd. From Warmsley's to Ogdens Cole (sic) *House to Join Mr. DeWitt.*
4¾ x 5.
(47) ROAD TO MORRISTOWN BY MR. LOTTS.
13½ x 15. Small insert of homes of the inhabitants.
(48) *1st. From Rockaway Bridge to Horse Neck.*
7¾ x 13½.
2nd. Road from Peter Schuylers to the Forks and Horse Neck at Henry Pierce's & from the Forks to Totoway Bridge, Past the Great Falls to the Passaick.
17¼ x 19¼.
(49) CONTRACTION FROM QUAKER HILL TO HARTFORD. (missing)
(50A) ROAD THROUGH PEEKSKILL HOLLOW.
13 x 16.
B. *Road Through Peekskill Hollow &c.*
14¼ x 14½.
(51) FROM NEAR NEW WINDSOR THROUGH CHESTER TO MACE'S TAVERN.
22½ x 27. Irregular in shape, composed of several smaller sheets.
(52) See under *William Gray*.
(53) FROM RINGWOOD TO LONGPOND AND LOWER FORGE.
13¼ x 16¼.

The following were made during 1779:
(54) GENERAL CONTRACTION (4 MILES TO AN INCH) BY R. ERSKINE. LITCHFIELD, CONN. TO THE NAVESINK HIGHLANDS.
17½ x 24½. Carefully finished, formalized draft on a grid with borders. This is a finished draft of map B part 1.
(55) See under *William Scull*.
(56) ROADS FROM POMPTON, PARAMUS, GREAT FALLS &C.
A. *From Pond's Church to Paramus, Totowa, Pompton.* 12¾ x 16.

B. *Roads from Pompton, Paramus, Great Falls &c. (2nd part)* 14½ x 19. Irregular elongation of sheet at lower end.

(57) ROAD FROM BETHLEHEM TO BROAD AX AND CHESTNUT HILL, PENNSYLVANIA.

A. *Road from Leak's Ferry toward Philadelphia.* 11¼ x 17¼.

B. *From Martin Conrad's past Tohicken Church toward Philadelphia.* 13¾ x 17½.

C. *From Jacob Mires to the Green Tree Tavern.* 9½ x 12.

D. *From Green Tree Tavern to the Broad Axe Tavern.* 11 x 19.

E. *From Broad Axe to Chestnut Hill.* 8¾ x 15½.

(58) FROM BETHLEHEM TO BROAD AXE.

9¼ x 33½.

(59) ROADS ABOUT WHITE PLAINS. (attached to No. 120)

16 x 26. *Near the White Plains across from Sawmill River toward the Brunks to near Thos. Thompsons.* 4¼ x 5¼.

(60) ABOUT WHITE PLAINS.

19 x 25¾.

(62) DRAUGHT OF THE SOUTHERN COAST OF LAKE ERIE; A & B, A CONTRACTION OF D⁰. (missing)

(63) MAP OF NIAGRA R. ON THE STRAITS BETWEEN ERIE AND ONTARIO. (missing).

(64) MAP OF THE SHIP CHANNEL ON LAKE ST. CLAIRE. (missing).

(65) PART OF THE SUSQUEHANA & DELAWARE-ONO-NOUGHQUA &C. (missing).

(66) See under *Simeon DeWitt.*

(67) ROAD FROM FORKS PASSAIC TO SCOTCH PLAINS.

A. *From Pompton towards West . . . By the Forks and Little Falls.* 10½ x 15½.

B. *From Springfield through Watseking to Newark Mountains.* 12¼ x 15¼.

C. *Through Scotch Plains & Springfield.* 12 x 14¾.

D. *From Quibbletown towards Scotch Plains.* 7¼ x 12.

D. part 2. 7 x 12.

(68) ROAD FROM EASTON TO CHESTER.

21½ x 27¼.

(69) FROM NEAR CHESTER TO BETHLEHEM.

1st. 13 x 14¼.
2nd. 13 x 16.
3rd. 13¼ x 16.
4th. 13 x 15½.
5th. 12¾ x 15.
6th. 13¼ x 15½.
7th. 13½ x 14.
8th. 15 x 30¼. Irregular, of three sheets.
9th. 13 x 15¾. Town of Easton.
10th. 12½ x 16. Bethlehem.

(70) ROAD FROM DUYCKINKS MILL TO GERMANTOWN.

A. *Road from Mr. Ten Eykes toward Germantown, past the Clothier General.* 11 x 14.

B. *Roads from Cross Roads through Pluckemin toward Morristown.* 12½ x 15½.

C. *Road toward Morristown past Baskingridge Meeting House; and joined Mr. McMurray's work near Woodward's Mill. Another Road beginning at John Bibouts', thence towards Quibbletown, crossing the Dead River.* 12¼ x 15.

D. *Road from Mount Bethel Meeting House to near Quibbletown and from Quibbletown to Brunswick.* 12 x 15¼.

E. *Road from Brunswick to Boundbrook.* 12 x 15.

F. *Road from Boundbrook to Mr. Ten Eyck continued.* 12¼ x 14¼.

(71) ROAD FROM DUYCKINKS' MILL TO THE SOUTH, BOTH SIDES OF THE RIVER.

A. 9½ x 15.

B. *Road from Garrison's Tavern to Somerset Ct. Hᴱ and from Somerset to Van Nep's Mill & from Van Nep's Mill to Boundbrook.* 11 x 15.

C. *From near Head Quarters where the Road goes to the Dikins Mills, toward Morrell's Tavern & joins the Road surveyed from Mor-*

rell's Tavern to Matthew Tanckes on the East Side of the Branch. 7½ x 9.

(72) FROM DUYCKINK'S MILL TO THE WHITE HOUSE, POTTERSTOWN, GERMANTOWN, LAMATUNCK.

A. *Road from near B. Tavern to the White House.* 11¼ x 13.

B. *Road from the White House to Potterstown & from Potterstown to Germantown, thence towards Lamertunk Meeting House.*

(73) FROM SKEEPACK ROAD, CROSS CORRIELL'S FERRY TO MORRISTOWN.

1st. *From Skeepack Road near Weaver's Tav'n. The Swede Fork Road to near Doyles Tavern toward Morristown.* 12½ x 15½.

2nd. *From near Doyles Tavern, Swedes Fork Road into the old York Road & along it towards Morristown.* 12¼ x 15¼.

3rd. *Crossing Corrells Ferry toward Morristown to Ringo's Tavern.* 13¼ x 20¾.

4th. *From near Ringoes, crossing Newshannock River and the South Branch of Raritan toward Morristown.* 13¾ x 21.

5th. *Past the White House to the Crossroads, towards Morristown, crossing Lamatunck River.* 15 x 21½.

6th. *From the Cross-roads crossing the North Branch of Raritan to near Vealtown, towards Morristown.* 12¼ x 15¼.

7th. *Through Vealtown to Morristown.* 12½ x 14.

(74) FROM BOUND BROOK, QUIBBLETOWN . . . ELIZABETHTOWN ETC.

A. 11 x 15¼.

B. *Road from the Short Hills to Wheat Sheaf, on the Post Road.* 11¾ x 15¼.

C. *From Wheat Sheaf on the York Post Road to Elizabethtown.* 12 x 14.

D. *Road from the Wheat Sheaf thro' Woodbridge to Amboy & from Amboy towards Brunswick.* 12 x 15.

E. *Road from the Third Forking Paths thro' Bonumtown & Piscataway to Brunswick.* 11¾ x 15.

F. *Road from Brunswick thro' Somerset to Van Vacter's Bridge.* 12 x 14¾.

(75) ROAD FROM NEAR MORRISTOWN THROUGH BOTTLE HILL AND CHATHAM TOWARDS SPRINGFIELD.

A. *Road from near Morristown through Bottle Hill and Chatham towards Springfield. Irregular shape.* 12¼ x 14¾.

B. *Road from Springfield to Elizabethtown. Irregular shape.* 12¼ x 14¾.

C. *Road from Raway Meeting House to Westfield, from Westfield towards the Short Hills.* 11½ x 11½.

(76) ROAD FROM HEADQUARTERS TO MIDDLEBROOK, PLUCKAMIN &C. (missing).

(77) ROADS FROM POTTERSTOWN, HICKORY TAVERN, MUSCANECUNK MOUNTAIN, REDDINGTON, JOHNSON'S FORGE, EASTON: A.B.C.D FROM LETTER B TO THE ROAD FROM CORRIELL'S TO MORRISTOWN; E FROM NEAR HENRY CAMP'S ON THE ROAD FROM CORRIELL'S TO MORRISTOWN TO REDDINGTON.

A. *From Potterstown towards Hickory Tavern.* 13 x 16.

B. *Road from towards Potterstown past the Hickory Tavn. towards Reddington.* 9¾ x 15.

C. *From Muscanecunk Mountain Past Johnson's Forge to Easton.* 12¼ x 15.

D. *From Letter B (on Nᵒ 77C) to the Road from Corrells to Morristown.* 13 x 16¼.

E. *From near Henry Camps to Riddington.* 7½ x 7½. (attached to 77D).

(78) FROM SHORT HILLS TAVᴺ TO SPANKTOWN AND CRAIG'S TAVERN.

13 x 15½.

(79) See under *Benjamin Lodge.*

(80) FROM NEAR GARRISON'S TAVᴺ TO PAST GEN'L HEARD'S & FROM NEAR HEARD'S TO PRINCETON, SOMERSET, THROUGH KINGSTON.

1st & 2nd sheets. (missing).

(81) ROUGH CONTRACTION IN THE JERSEYS.
8 miles to an inch. 8¼ x 13¼.

(82) FROM ELIZABETH TOWN POINT TO TOTOWA.
11½ x 14.

(83) CONTRACTION TO EASTON & CORIELL'S FERRY.
4 miles to 1 inch. (missing).

(84A) ROAD FROM WIDOW VANAMBROSE'S TO THE FOREST OF DEAN AND THENCE TWO ROADS, VIZ, ONE TO CLEMAN'S SAW-MILL & THE OTHER TO NEAR WEST POINT.
13 x 16. There is a note on one elevation: "Has a fine Prospect from this Hill could see the River near Peekskill likewise the Hill I do suppose mostly called Anthony's nose."
B. Unfinished. 15 x 20¼.

(85) FROM SMITH'S CLOVE TO CHESTER. (missing).

(86) FROM JUNE'S TO ARCHER AND WARWICK.
A. *From Junes to Archies.* 11 x 13½.
B. 11¾ x 12.
B. 2nd. 14½ x 20½.

(87) ROADS FROM NEAR SOMERSET COURT HOUSE BY PENNYTOWN TO THE DIFFERENT FERRYS TO TRENTON, TO BRISTOL, PHILADELPHIA, COOPER'S FERRY, MOUNT HOLLY, ALLENTOWN, CRANBURY & BRUNSWICK; A, B, C, D, E, F, G; & H; & FROM CHESTNUT HILL TO PHILADELPHIA.
A. *Road from Ram Garrison's to Near Pennytown.* 15 x 10½. "A Rough Stony uneven Road almost all the way".
B. *Road from Pennytown to Slack's Ferry and from Dº to Trenton and Howell's Ferries.* 12¾ x 20¼.
C. *Road from Trenton Ferry to Bristol.* 13¼ x 16½.
D. *Road from Bristol to Kingsington.* 21 x 29¼.
E. *Road from upper end of Kingsington to Market House in Philadelphia, and from thence two others, viz; from Market House to Falls of Schuylkill and from Cooper's Ferry past the 14 M. stone from Burlington.* 13¾ x 20.
F. *Road from near the 14 M. S. from Burlington thro Moorstown & to one James Sippingwills.* 21 x 30.
G. *Road from James Sippingwills thro. Slattown, Black Horse, Crosswicks, Allentown, Hightstown and Cranbury to near Cross Road.* 21 x 29.

(90A) ROAD FROM POMPTON BY THE WARWICK ROAD TO MORRISTOWN, UP POMPTON RIVER PAST CHARLOTTEBURG IRON WORKS.
13¾ x 21¼.
B. *Road from near Genᴸ Wines to Morristown and from SD. road to Boonton thence down the Rockaway River until it joins a road surveyed by Mr. Lodge.* 15½ x 20.
C. *Road from the Sussex Road toward Morristown past Longwood, Burkshire, Beaman's and Mt. Pleasant Forges to Gen Waynes.* 18¾ x 26.

(91A) A ROUGH DRAUGHT OF THE ROAD FROM EASTON TO WYOMING CONTRACTED FROM A SCALE OF 2 MILES TO AN INCH.
20¾ x 27.
B. *Road from Northumberland in the Jerseys to Wyoming.* 13 x 29.

(92A) ROAD FROM WYOMING TOWARD TIOGA, ACROSS THE LACKAWANNA TOWARDS TIMHANNOCK.
13 x 16¼.
B. *Road from Wyoming towards Tioga continued past Timhannock.* 13 x 15¾.
C. (missing).
D. *Road from Easton to Wyoming continued.* 13½ x 14.
E. *Road from Easton to Wyoming continued.* 12¼ x 15½.
F. *Road from Easton to Wyoming continued.* 13¼ x 16½.
G. *Road from Easton to Wyoming continued past Bullock's House.* 12½ x 15½.
H. *This sheet comes to Wyoming.* 7½ x 12¼.
J. & K. (missing).
L. *Road from Wyoming towards Tioga past Wialusing.* 13 x 16.
M. *Road from Wialusing towards Tioga past Wisawken Creek to*

Upper Shesekemunk Flats where the army encamped. 13¼ x 16¼.

(93) FROM NEWBORROUGH TO ALBANY AND FROM ALBANY TO FISHKILL.
A. *From Newborough towards Albany.* 9¾ x 16¼.
B. *From Newborough towards Albany continued.* 8½ x 15¾.
C. *From Newborough towards Albany.* 8½ x 16½.
D. *From Newborough towards Albany to Kingston.* 10¼ x 16¼.
E. *From Kingston toward Albany.* 13 x 16¾.
F. *Between Kingston & Albany.* 13¼ x 16½.
G. *Between Kingston thro. Catskill.* 13 x 16½.
H. *Between Kingston & Albany thro' Kooksakie.* 13 x 16½.
I. *Between Kingston & Albany through Kolymans.* 13½ x 16½.
K. *Between Kingston & Albany past Van Wies.* 13¼ x 16½.
L. *From Albany towards Fishkill.* 13¼ x 16½.
M. *Between Albany and Kinderhook.* 13½ x 16½.
N. *Between Albany & Fishkill thro' Kinderhook.* 13¼ x 16.
O. *Between Albany and Fishkill thro' Clavrack.* 13¼ x 16¼.
P. *Between Albany and Fishkill to the Red Hook.* 13½ x 16½.
Q. *Between Albany and Fishkill thro' the Red Hook.* 13¼ x 16½.
R. *Between Albany and Fishkill thro' Rhynbeck.* 13¼ x 16½.
S. *Between Albany and Fishkill.* 13¼ x 16¾.
T. *Between Albany and Fishkill through Poughkeepsie.* 13¼ x 16½.
U. *Between Albany and Fishkill to the Town of Fishkill.* 13 x 16½.
V. *From Fishkill to Newborough.* 13½ x 16¼.

(94) CONTRACTION OF ABOVE FROM ALBANY TO NEWBOROUGH & FISHKILL. (missing).

(95A) ROAD FROM THE FORKS OF THE RIVER SUSQUEHANNA TOWᴰ WYOMING.
B. *Road from the Forks of Susquehanna to Wyoming continued.* 12¼ x 14¾.
C. *From Forks of Susquehanna toward Wyoming.* 12½ x 15¼.
D. *From Forks of Susquehanna to Wyoming. Irregular shape.* 13 x 15.
E. *From the Forks towᴰ Wyoming.* 7¼ x 13.
F. *From the Forks of Susquehanna towᴰ Wyoming.* 13 x 16.
G. *From the Forks toward Wyoming.* 8¼ x 13¾.
H. *From the Forks towards Wyoming continᴰ past Shickohonna.* 8¼ x 13¾.
I. *From the Forks of Susquehanna towᴰ Wyoming past Nanticoke Falls.* 13¼ x 16¼.
K. *Road from Forks of Susquehanna to Wyoming concluded.* 13¼ x 16½.

(96) ROUT FROM FORT SULLIVAN TO CHEMING & TO NEWTON.
A. *From Fort Sullivan past Chemung.* 13½ x 16½.
B. *Past Newton to Catharine's town.* 13¼ x 16½.
B. 2nd. *This sheet joins B 96 at Fort Reed where the road to Chinnesee leaves the Cayuga Branch.* 13¼ x 16½.
C. *From Catherinestown down Seneca Lake.* 13¼ x 16½.
D. *Down the Seneca Lake past Condy or Appleton.* 13 x 16½.
E. *To the Outlet of Seneca Lake.* 8¼ x 9.
F. *Road across the outlet of Seneca Lake.* 8¼ x 11.
G. *Up the Cayuga Lake past Chonodote.* 9 x 16½.
H. *To the upper end of Cayuga Lake.* 12 x 16½.
I. *From the Head at the Lake towards Newton.* 13¼ x 16½.
K. *To the place adjoining Newton.* 8½ x 13¼.

(97) FROM SENECA LAKE TO CHENISSEE.
A. *Thro' Cannadisago towards Chinnissee past Kassandogne.* 8 x 16¾.
B. *Thro' Haunyauya towards Chinisee.* 11½ x 16½.
C. *To Chinnissee Castle.* 7¼ x 16¾.

(98 and 99) See under *William Scull.*

(100) SPHERICAL PROJECTIONS.
1st. *Unfinished spherical projection* locating Amboy, Elizabethtown, Chester, N. Y. and New York-New Jersey border. 19½ x 31½.
2nd. is just a grid.

(101) FROM HARTFORD, NEW HAVEN, NORWALK, BEDFORD &C.
A, B, C, D, E. (missing).

(102) CONTRACTION FROM HARTFORD, NEW HAVEN, NOR-
WALK, BEDFORD &C 4 MILES AN INCH.
Carefully executed detailed survey within geographical border. 17¾
x 24. In lower right corner, "Robt. Erskine F.R.S. Del^T 1779".
The following were done in 1780:
(103) See under *Benjamin Lodge*.
(104) ROADS ABOUT CAMP AT MORRISTOWN A, B, C, D &
E. FROM NEAR CHATHAM TO HORSENECK.
A. *Road from Kembles to Chatham.* 21¼ x 21½.
B. *Road from Morristown thro' Jockey Hollow.* 12 x 12¾.
C. *From Bottle Hill towards Newark past Mountain Meeting Place.*
15 x 20½.
D. *Road from Norris's Tower in Morristown past the Park of Artillery to Gen'l Knox's Quarters.* 5½ x 12.
E. *Road from Chatham to Horseneck.* 14½ x 19½.
(105) SURVEY OF MORRISTOWN BY THE CHAIN ONLY, BY
R. ERSKINE.
12½ x 20.
(106) See under *Simeon DeWitt*.
(107) ROAD BETWEEN CHATHAM, SCOTCH PLAINS, TUR-
KEY AND SPRINGFIELD.
13 x 13¼.
(108) FROM COL. DAY'S TO THE PONDS, & FROM WYKOFF
TO BELLEGROVE.
14 x 20¾.
(109) FROM LITTLE FALLS TO ACQUACKNUCK. (missing).
(110) FROM DOBBS FERRY TO PERAMES.
14¾ x 21½.
(111) CONTRACTIONS IN THE JERSEYS (12 MILES TO AN
INCH) AMBOY, BRUNSWICK, PLUCKEMIN, MORRISTOWN,
NEWFOUNDLAND, CHARLOTTEBURG, PARAMUS, BY R. E.
(missing).
(112) WIDTH OF N.R. (NORTH RIVER) AT CLOSTER A;
AND B AT DOBBS FERRY MEASURED WITH A THEODOLITE BY
R. E. (missing).
B. *Data for ascertaining the width of the North River at Dobbs
Ferry taken with a Theodolite July 17th 1780 by Robt. Erskine FRS
Geog^R AUS.* 8¼ x 12. Identical map forwarded in a letter from
General Wayne to Washington, July 18, 1780. Washington Manuscripts, Library of Congress (39, 183).
(113) ROADS BETWEEN SUFFRANS, TAPPAN, KAKEATE,
PARAMUS, DOBBS FERRY, CLARKSTOWN &C.
1st sheet. 19¼ x 25¼.
2nd sheet. *From Haverstraw Forge tow^D Suffrans.* 14 x 21½.
(114) CONTRACTIONS OF D^O & SUNDRY PLACES RECTIFIED.
(missing). This is the last entry in Erskine's hand. He died October
2, 1780.

18. FRANCOIS DE FLEURY

Francois Louis Teisseidre de Fleury was a native of St. Hippolyte, Languedoc Province, France. After nine years of service in the French Army, at the age of 28, he departed for
America on the "Amphitrite" on February 14, 1777 in company with a group of engineers, including Tronson du Coudray.
The Committee on French Applications dispatched him to
Washington on May 22 as a Captain of Engineers. Fleury distinguished himself in the Battle of Brandywine but suffered the
loss of his horse. In the same battle, his fellow traveler du
Coudray lost his life. Because of Fleury's gallantry, Congress
passed a resolution to supply him with another horse.

On October 3, 1777, Fleury was appointed Brigade-Major to
Pulaski and distinguished himself in the Battle of Germantown
in which he was wounded. He was then assigned as an engineer to Fort Mifflin on Mud Island below Philadelphia and
was wounded again in the defense of the Fort.

On November 26, 1777, Fleury was promoted to Lieutenant
Colonel of Engineers. He remained with the army at Valley
Forge, participated in the Battle of Monmouth the following
spring and in the retreat from Rhode Island in August. He
again distinguished himself in the assault on Stony Point on the
Hudson. For his outstanding courage, Fleury was awarded a
special medal, the only one given a foreign officer during the
Revolution. Fleury was granted leave on September 27, 1779
and returned to France. There he terminated his service in the
American Army. However, he returned to America as an officer in the French Army under the command of Rochambeau
and served for the remainder of the War. Subsequently, Fleury
served in French India as Commander of the Regiment of Pondichery and as Governor of the Islands of Mauritius and Bourbon in the Indian Ocean. He returned to France in April 1790
and participated in the Battles of Montmedy, Valenciennes and
Mons. In the last battle he was injured and he left the Army on
June 24, 1792.

From a bibliographic point of view, material on Fleury
may be found occasionally under "Henry" because of a mis-
interpretation of his manuscript hand.

(1) "A SKETCH OF THE SIEGE OF FORT SCHUYLER PRE-
SENTED TO COL. GANSEVOORT BY L. FLEURY."
September 1777. A 19th century manuscript copy of the original
made for Jared Sparks by G. H. Bowen. 11 x 16¼. Sparks Collection,
Cornell University Library. MPI 553.

(2) "A SKETCH OF THE SIEGE OF FORT SCHUYLER PRE-
SENTED TO COL. GANSEVOORT BY L. FLURY (SIC)."
A manuscript copy on handmade paper. 11 x 15¾. New York Public
Library, Manuscript Collection.
   Note: The location of the original from which the two preceding
   were made is unknown. The second sketch of Fort Schuyler
   with Fleury misspelled is reproduced in *Annals of Tryon
   County* by William Campbell and in the *Life of Joseph
   Brant* by William L. Stone, printed in 1831 and 1838 in
   New York. The circumstances of Fleury's authorship are
   unknown. The map itself shows the important portage connecting Wood Creek which flowed into Lake Ontario and
   the Mohawk River which enters the Hudson. This was the
   strategic reason for the Fort and its predecessor, Fort Newport.

(3) MUDD ISLAND.
A manuscript survey with narrow borders showing the west shore of
the Delaware River, Mud Island and Hog Island. 15 x 18½. Detailed
renditions of the armaments, lines of fire, chevaux de frise, channels,
etc. Sparks Collection, Cornell University Library. MPI 535.

(4) "FIGURE APROXIMATIF DU FORT MIFFLIN DES OUV-
RAGES DES ASSIEGEANS 9TH 9BRE 1777."
A detailed ms. in border, 13 x 16¼ in larger scale and greater detail
than the preceding. On the opposite side is written "Major Fleury's
Plan of Fort Mifflin", "the engineer officer of this imperfect draft
begg indulgence for it; Considering the he has not paper, pen, rule
neither cercel, and being disturbed by good many shells or Cannon's
balls flying in the fort." Sparks Collection, Cornell University Library.
MPI 536.

(5) "FIGURE APROXIMATIF DES OUVRAGES DES ASSIEGEANS
14 9BRE 1777."
A rough ms. without border showing the western portion of Fort Mif-
lin and the immediately adjacent Pennsylvania shore. 14 x 17. It is
addressed to "his excellency General Washington headquarter". Sparks
Collection, Cornell University Library. MPI 537.

(6) "FIGURE APROXIMATIF DE FORT ISLAND & DES OUV-
RAGES DES ASSIEGEANS 16 OCTOBRE 1777."
A ms. 8 x 13 very much like the preceding but more detailed. On the
opposite side is a long explanatory note. Sparks Collection, Cornell
University Library. MPI 534.

(7) "VIEW OF THE ENEMY FLEET BEFORE PHILADELPHIA 19 JANUARY 1778."
A ms. 7 x 9½ with the names of the British vessels and sent to Washington by the author. Sparks Collection, Cornell University Library. MPI 547.

19. ALEXANDER FRASER

Alexander Fraser, a native of South Carolina, was commissioned a 2nd Lieutenant in the First South Carolina Regiment on January 31, 1778 and was promoted to 1st Lieutenant October 6, 1778. He participated in the Battle of Savannah. When the American defenders were outflanked at Charleston, Fraser was taken prisoner on May 12, 1780 some weeks prior to the battle.
BATTLE OF SAVANNAH. DEC. 29, 1778 A. FRASER-FECIT.
A crude ms. without scale. 13 x 15. New York Historical Society.

20. JEAN-BAPTISTE DE GOUVION

Jean-Baptiste de Gouvion was born January 8, 1747 at Toul, France. He was the son of a councillor. He was commissioned a 2nd Lieutenant at the engineering school at Mezieres January 1, 1769, promoted to 1st Lieutenant January 1, 1771 and later became a Captain. He came to America in company with Duportail, Radiere and Laumoy, his service starting on January 25, 1777 with the rank of Major of Engineers.

Gouvion's initial task was aiding Duportail and later he was active in planning the works at West Point. He was promoted to Lt. Colonel on November 17, 1777. Following the capture of Stony Point by the Americans, he constructed the redoubt on the opposite shore of the Hudson River at Verplank's Point. He was promoted to Colonel on November 16, 1781 shortly after he made his map of Yorktown.

Gouvion retired from the American Army on October 10, 1783 and returned to France where he continued to serve the French Army with steady promotion until he finally became Marechal de Camp on June 30, 1791. He was elected a Deputy to the French Assembly in 1792 but was wounded at Glisuelle on June 11 of that year and died shortly thereafter.
PLAN OF THE ATTACK OF YORK IN VIRGINIA BY THE ALLIED ARMIES AND FRANCE COMMANDED BY HIS EXCELLENCY GENERAL WASHINGTON, HIS EXCELLENCY THE COUNT ROCHAMBEAU COMMANDING THE FRENCH ARMY OCTOBER 29, 1781.
A finished, somewhat irregularly shaped colored map 29 x 38 with extensive descriptive notes. This was sent to the President of Congress by Washington. National Archives.

21. WILLIAM GRAY

William Gray was appointed a 1st Lieutenant in the First Battalion of Miles Pennsylvania Rifle Regiment March 15, 1776. He was captured at the Battle of Long Island August 27, 1776 and exchanged December 8. Gray was promoted to Captain of the Fourth Pennsylvania Regiment on January 3, 1777 and retired from service, still a Captain, on January 17, 1781. He died July 18, 1804.

Gray's cartographic contribution was a series of manuscript maps made in 1778 under orders of Robert Erskine, the Geographer of the American Army. These were of Col. William Butler's line of march against the Iroquois at Unadilla and elsewhere and are recorded as Number 52 in Erskine's list. The maps are the subject of a letter in the collection of the New York Historical Society.

(52) FROM ALBANY TO SCHOHARIE & CONTRACTION.
4 pieces by Capt. Gray.
A. *From Albany to Schoharie.* 1st Part.
sheet 1. 20 x 26½. (continued on next).
sheet 2. 20½ x 23.
B. *Albany to Schoharie.* 2nd Part. 19½ x 24. Scale 100 chains to an inch. Shows town of Duansburg and Cobes Kill.
C. *Albany to Schoharie.* 3rd Part.
1st piece. 15 x 32¾. Shows Albany, upper Hudson River, Mohawk River as does sheet 1 but on a smaller scale.
2nd piece. 13¼ x 16. 4 miles to an inch. The Susquehanna River, west branch of the Delaware River, path to Cherry Valley and the town of Onanaughquago.
3rd piece. Not labeled. Detail of two rails converging on a grist mill as shown on the western half of the 3rd part of the first piece.

The first four maps are on blue paper, the only ones so drawn in the entire Erskine-DeWitt series. This may be due to Gray's difficulty in obtaining materials as cited in his letter, mentioned previously.

22. JOHN GRENELL

John Grenell of Huntington, N. Y. was a Captain in the Suffolk County Company of the 3rd Regiment of Colonel James Clinton. He was ordered to duty to the fortifications in the Hudson Highlands on November 3, 1775. One month later he was relieved of these duties and made Captain of a company of matrosses or gunners. December 8, 1775 he was detailed to command an artillery company. Then on March 27 of the next year, Grenell resigned because of a disagreement over promotion of a subordinate.
(HUDSON RIVER HIGHLANDS) FROM POLYPHENES ISLAND AND BUTTER HILL, SOUTH TO LOWER END OF TAPPAN BAY BELOW DOBBS FERRY AND CORBETTS FERRY.
Carefully executed manuscript survey 14¾ x 30 showing soundings "Drawn by request and under the inspection of the Commissioners of Fortifications in the Highlands province of New York by John Grenell". "Scale of an inch & a half to a mile". "Soundings in fathoms". There is a table of distances. The map has had a lot of use. Sparks Collection, Cornell University Library. (MPI 526).

23. ADAM HUBLEY, JR.

Adam Hubley, Jr. was born in 1744 and was active in public affairs in the Lancaster area. He joined the 1st Pennsylvania Battalion as a 1st Lieutenant on October 27, 1775. He served in various grades in Pennsylvania troops. As a Lieutenant Colonel and having served in the Battles of Brandywine, Germantown and Whitemarsh, Hubley commanded the 11th Pennsylvania Regiment on June 5, 1779.

Hubley was assigned to General Hand's brigade during Sullivan's expedition against the Indians of Western New York. During this, Hubley kept a personal journal which contains the following sketch maps of the encampments. He retired on January 1, 1781 from the military. Later he served in the State Assembly and Senate. Hubley died in Philadelphia in the Yellow Fever epidemic in 1793 and was buried in St. Peter's Cemetery.

All the following manuscript sketch maps are in one of Hubley's two small military journals in the Historical Society of Pennsylvania. One volume is concerned with military organization and the other is an account of General John Sullivan's expedition against the Indians of Western New York in 1779. The latter contains also sketches of Indian monuments, houses, etc. Hubley commanded the 11th Pennsylvania Regiment in the Sullivan operation.

The journals and maps were the subject of an excellent study by John W. Jordan in the "Pennsylvania Magazine of History and Biography" volume XXXIII, 1909.

(1) A Sketch of the Encampment of Wyoming.
5¾ x 7½.
(2) A Sketch of the Encampment of Lackawanay.
4¼ x 5¾.
(3) Sketch of the Encampment at Quialutemunk.
5¾ x 7½.
(4) Sketch of the Tunkhunnunk Encampment.
5½ x 5¾.
(5) Sketch of Encampment at Wyalussing.
5¾ x 7½.
(6) Sketch of Encampment at Wesenking.
5¾ x 7½.
(7) Sketch of Encampment at Sheshecununk.
4 x 5¾.
(8) Sketch of Encampment and Works on Tioga Plains.
5¾ x 7½.
(9) Course &c of Susquehanna (North East Branch) from Wyoming to the Mouth of Tiogo.
Excellent, careful map on folding page. 11½ x 15½.
(10) Sketch of Fort Sullivan, August 12th, 1779.
(Blank page).
(11) Camps on Upper & Lower Chemung and Camp on Tioga Branch together folding sheet.
8¾ x 13¼.
(12) Sketch of Encampment and Adjacent Country, Upper End of Tioga Flatts Alias Kanedohauraughwe.
5¾ x 6.
(13) Sketch of Encampment at Entrance of Defile Near Chemung.
5¾ x 7½.
(14) Sketch of Encampment at Chemung.
5¾ x 7½.
(15) Sketch of Encampment Near Newtown Aug^T 29th.
5¾ x 7½.
(16) Order of Encampment This Night (August 31).
5¾ x 5.
(17) Sketch of Encampment at Catherines-town.
5¾ x 7½.
(18) Sketch of Encampment September 3^D.
5¼ x 5.
(19) Sketch of Encampment This Night.
(September 4th).
3¼ x 5¾.
(20) Sketch of Encampment at Candai.
5¾ x 7½.
(21) Sketch of Encampment Near Candai.
5¾ x 7½.
(22) Sketch of Our Encampment at Kanadaraga.
5¾ x 7½.
(23) Sketch of Encampment, This Evening (September 10th).
3¾ x 5¾.
(24) Sketch of Encampment (September 11th).
5 x 5¾.
(25) Sketch of Encampment, This Night (September 12th).
5¾ x 6.
(26) Sketch of Encampment at Gaglisuguilakeny.
5¾ x 7½.

(27) Sketch of Encampment at Ienise.
5½ x 5¾.
(28) Sketch of Encampment This Night (September 15th).
3½ x 5¾.
(29) Sketch of Encampment This Night (September 16th).
5¾ x 7½.
(30) Sketch of Encampment This Night (September 18th).
5¾ x 6.
(31) Sketch of Encampment This Night (September 19th).
4 x 5¾.
(32) Sketch of Encampment This Night (September 21st).
4 x 5¾.
(33) Sketch of Encampment This Night (September 22nd).
5¾ x 7½.
(34) Sketch of Encampment at Vanderlip's & Williams Farm.
5½ x 5¾.

24. Gilles-Jean Kermorvan

Gilles-Jean Barazer Chevalier Kermorvan was born December 23, 1740 of a Breton family in the Cote-du-Nord, France. He was commissioned a Lieutenant in the regiment of Bre' June 20, 1758 and later served as an engineer in the war between Russia and Turkey.

Kermorvan was one of the earliest French volunteers to arrive in America when he came to Philadelphia in June 1776. His first assignment was to lay out military works on the New Jersey shore at Billingsport for the defense of Philadelphia. Kermorvan was appointed Lieutenant-Colonel of Engineers on July 16 and ordered to Perth Amboy. A short time later he made up the following plan for coastal defense (apparently a map) which was forwarded to John Hancock. Unfortunately the letter, plan and accompanying draughts have been lost.

Kermorvan served with distinction with Morgan's riflemen in the campaign which ended with Burgoyne's surrender. Unable to obtain a promotion, he resigned and returned to France in 1778. He later attained high rank in the French Republican army and died in 1817.

Un Plan General Pour la Defense Des Cotes de l'Amerique Mentioned in a Letter to Benjamin Franklin from Perth Amboy Dated July 26, 1776. The receipt of the letter "with a plan and draughts" is recorded but their location is unknown.

25. Henry Knox

Henry Knox, born in Boston July 25, 1750, was a man of many talents. He was the son of a ship master who died when Henry was 12. Knox worked in the book trade from an early age and at 21 started his own book store which soon prospered. He not only purveyed but read his wares, particularly technical works and those on the developing science of artillery.

By 1770 Knox had enlisted in the local militia company and in 1772 became second in command of the Boston Grenadier Corps. With the start of the Revolution, he was commissioned a Colonel November 17, 1775. He recognized the importance of filling the near void in American artillery and journeyed to Ticonderoga where he secured a large number of captured pieces. Much of the artillery was large and heavy and the roads between Ticonderoga and Boston had never been subjected to such loads. Despite this, Knox brought the artillery through in record time. Use of this artillery in fortifying Dorchester Heights forced the evacuation of Boston by the British under Howe.

The success of Knox's venture brought him to the attention of Washington. He fought in the Battles of Long Island and Trenton and probably made the sketch map of the latter battle area on the verso of the general orders.

On December 17, 1776, Knox was elevated to Brigadier General. In addition to participating in the Battles of Brandywine and Monmouth, he became Chief of Artillery and suggested the establishment of the Government Arsenal at Springfield, Massachusetts. He was in command of the fortifications at West Point and dependencies, and suggested the establishment of a national military academy.

Knox was promoted to Major General on November 15, 1781. After Yorktown, in which he took an active part, he conceived and organized The Society of the Cincinnati and served as its first secretary. He finally resigned from the Army in January 1784.

In civilian life, Knox became an active speculator in real estate in Maine and was appointed to settle the differences with the Penobscot Indians. His home at Thomaston, Maine, was the most magnificent mansion north of Boston; and his princely scale of living usually kept him in debt. The General who had been physically large in youth, grew with success to an eventual 300 pounds. Together with his nearly equally obese wife, he was the center of interest and activity on the then primitive Maine Coast. Knox served as Secretary of War from 1785 to 1794 and died in 1806.

MAP OF THE AMERICAN CAMP AT MORRISTOWN AND SURROUNDING COUNTRYSIDE.
A crude ms. of the region bounded by Arthur Kill, the Raritan River, the Morristown area and Newark. It shows the location of the camp of the American troops, roads and communities. 11¼ x 16. The map accompanied a letter from Knox to Colonel Henry Jackson dated Morristown March 23, 1777 which, however, does not mention the map specifically. Boston Public Library.

26. ANDREW KOSCIUSZKO

Andrew Thaddeus Bonaventure Kosciuszko was born in Poland in 1746 and was educated in the military academy in Warsaw. In addition to pursuing his military subjects, he also studied for a year at the Academie Royal de Peinture et de Sculpture in Paris.

Kosciuszko left Europe at the end of June 1776, arriving in America by the end of August. He was appointed to the Engineer Corps with the rank of Colonel on August 30, 1776 and took part in the Saratoga Campaign, fortifying Bemis Heights as Head of Engineers in Gates' Army. Later he played a part in the fortification of West Point and encountered much friction with Radiere who had the same assignment. In 1780 he distinguished himself in the Carolina campaign under Greene.

Kosciuszko returned to Europe after the War but maintained his American friendships and was a member of the American Philosophical Society. A champion of independence, he lead Poland's unsuccessful rebellion against the Germans and Russians in 1794 and was imprisoned until 1796. After his release he returned briefly to the United States and France and died in Solothurn, Switzerland in 1817.

(1) (PLAN OF THE BATTLE OF SARATOGA).
A rough but accurate sketch showing elevations. 11¼ x 14. Zamoyski Library, Warsaw (present location unknown).
(2) "COL⁰ KOSKIASKO'S MAP OF WEST POINT."
A rough but well executed sketch map of the area. 13½ x 16½. Enclosed in a letter from Kosciuszko to General Alexander McDougall dated April 25, 1779 which in part says "I send you a ruff map of West Point" and containing an explanatory legend. New York Historical Society.
(3) (PLAN OF A REDOUBT AT WEST POINT).
A crude manuscript sketch which may have been part of the above. New York Historical Society.
(4) (A PLAN OF WEST POINT).
A manuscript map 28 x 31½ cm. On back is note: "This plan from the hand of General Thadeus Koscuiszko". The photostat in the New York Historical Society is 12½ x 14¾ and is labeled as "A Plan of West Point 1779—this plan belonged to Capt. Moses Greenleaf of the 11th Mass. Regt. who commanded Fort Putnam in the year 1779-80 S. Greenleaf". Massachusetts Historical Society.
(5) PLAN OF HALIFAX.
(Court House, N. C.) A crude pencil sketch 4 x 6½ showing army positions. Henry E. Huntington Library.

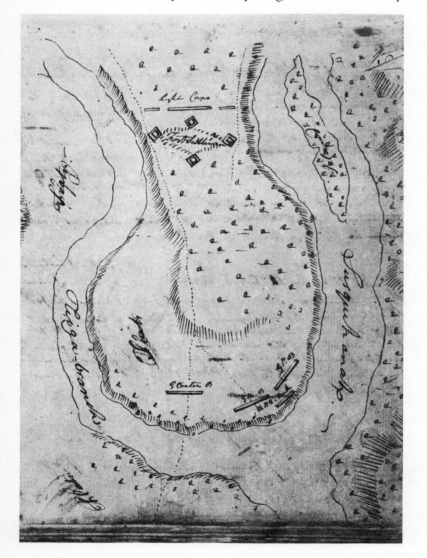

ADAM HUBLEY, JR. "Encampment at Tioga", from his journal. Hubley was an officer in the expedition under General John Sullivan against the Indians of Western New York. Historical Society of Pennsylvania.

27. BENJAMIN LODGE

Benjamin Lodge was commissioned an Ensign in the 12th Pennsylvania Regiment October 16, 1776, promoted to 2nd Lieutenant March 1, 1777, and to 1st Lieutenant October 11, 1777. He transferred to the 6th Pennsylvania July 1, 1778, and to the 3rd Pennsylvania January 1, 1783, and he served with the 3rd until June 3, 1783. He died in 1801.

Lodge's known maps are included in the Erskine-DeWitt series and are identified by their own numbers. All the surveys were made in 1779 and early 1780.

(79) FROM ELIZABETHTOWNPOINT, NEWARK, ACQUACKONONCK, WESEL, TOTOWA.

A. *From Elizabeth Town Point to Newark.* 11½ x 16¼. This bears the following "A most abominably Lazy slovenly performance not to survey such a small piece over again or lay it down properly, Witness R. E., F.R.S." Draught No. 75B.

B. *From Newark thro' Aquacknonk to Gotham.* 13¼ x 16½.

C. *From Gotham thro' Wesel to Totowa Bridge.* 11½ x 15¾.

(103) ROUTE OF THE WESTERN ARMY UNDER GEN'L SULLIVAN 1779.

A. *Route of the Western Army under Gen'l Sullivan.* 20½ x 29¾. Extends from the Delaware River to Buttermilk Creek, across the Pocono Mountains, upper Schuylkill River and the Susquehanna River.

A. *2nd Route of the Western Army, continued.* 20½ x 29½. From Nanticoke Creek to Sunbury.

A. *2nd Part. Route of the Western Army.* 14 x 19½. A partially completed plot on a careful grid extending from Lake Ontario and New York City, Philadelphia and New Jersey north of Barnegat Inlet.

B. *Route of the Western Army continued.* 21 x 29½. The Susquehanna River from Tunknunk Creek to Esther Town.

C. *Route of the Western Army continued.* 21 x 34. Lakes Cayuga and Seneca with the waterways draining them.

D. *Route of the Western Army continued.* 19½ x 29½. From "Chinnesee Castle", Adjutsa, Conyeadice, Haunyauya and Kanandaque Lake.

1ST ROUTE OF THE WESTERN ARMY.

Accurate uncompleted grid 21 x 29 with Lakes Seneca and Cayuga on the north to Wyoming and Sunbury on the south and east to the Hudson River. An excellent representation of the course of the rivers and streams.

28. CALEB LOWNES

Caleb Lownes was an engraver and die sinker who worked in the Philadelphia area in the last quarter of the 18th century. A Friend, he was a writer on prison reform including management and arrangements of prisons and was opposed to capital punishment. Lownes' single map is a plan of Boston Harbor. Lownes engraved the coat of arms of Pennsylvania in 1779.

A NEW PLAN OF BOSTON HARBOUR FROM AN ACTUAL SURVEY.

A careful copper engraving 7⅜ x 10¼ with a plan of the lines of the besieging American Army in the corner. One note "N.B. Charlestown Burnt, June 17, 1775, By the Regulars". Published in the *Pennsylvania Magazine* June 1775.

29. THOMAS MACHIN

Thomas Machin was born in England March 20, 1744 and settled in America in 1772. He was made a 2nd Lieutenant of the New York Artillery on January 18, 1776, and promoted to Captain Lieutenant in Lamb's 2nd Battalion of Artillery January 1, 1777. Machin was employed in construction and placement of at least one of the chains across the Hudson judging from the reference to a "Mr. Machin, Engineer" in a letter relating to the preparation of sites on each side of the river at Fort Montgomery to anchor the ends of the chain. Machin's map was made during this period of activity.

In 1779 Machin accompanied the expedition to the Genessee Country under command of Colonel Goose Van Schoick and General Clinton. He remained in service until 1783.

Machin settled at Newburgh and engaged in minting copper cents at the outlet from Orange Lake about 1787. Later he built adjoining grist and saw mills. He obtained large tracts of land in the northern part of Oneida County. He died April 3, 1816 at Charleston, Montgomery County, N. Y. Machin was a founding member of The Society of the Cincinnati and was succeeded by his son General Thomas Machin of Albany.

There are a few other early 19th century maps and surveys by Machin in the New York State Library but these are not included because of the stated limitation of this report to the Revolutionary War period. It should also be noted that a few inconsistencies were encountered in his military service history.

(THE HUDSON HIGHLANDS)

"To his Excellency George Clinton Esq.ᴿ Governoᴿ of the State of New York this map of Hudson's River through the Highlands is Humbly Dedicated by his Excellency's Most Humble Servant Thomas Machin IV January MDCCLXXVIII". A carefully executed, accurate and detailed map 13 x 46 by a somewhat untutored hand. There is a rectangular cartouche in the upper right corner containing the title. The map extends from just south of Newburgh to Kings Ferry. It shows in detail the roads, forts, homes of the inhabitants and the location of four obstructions to navigation. Sparks Collection, Cornell University Library. MPI 546.

30. WILLIAM MCMURRAY

William McMurray was commissioned a 2nd Lieutenant in Doyle's Independent Rifle Company July 17, 1776. He was promoted to 1st Lieutenant June 2, 1777. On July 1, 1778 he was transferred to the 10th Pennsylvania Regiment, and promoted to Captain April 1 the following year.

McMurray was transferred to the Sappers and Miners in 1780 but resigned in June of the following year. His one map was made during September 1780 but probably was not drafted until after the death of Robert Erskine, as it is numbered 123 in the Erskine-DeWitt series. Map 114 was the last made by Erskine a short time before his death on October 2, 1780.

THE SLOTE (4 CH. TO AN INCH) A PLAN OF THE SLOTE TAKEN SEPTEMBER 1780 WM. MCMURRAY CAPT.

An accurate careful survey within a border 14¼ x 15¾. "Scale of 16 perches to an inch". New York Historical Society.

Note: The term "Slote" was used as well as "Clove" to indicate a narrow cleft, gap or notch. The term was commonly applied to Smiths Clove in the Upper Ramapo Valley through which the principal road ran connecting New Windsor above the Hudson Highlands and the encampments in Northern New Jersey. The old route 17 and the New York Thruway pass through the "Clove".

31. LEWIS NICOLA

Lewis Nicola was born in France of Huguenot parents and was educated in Ireland. He emigrated from Dublin to Philadelphia in 1766 after 26 years of military service.

Nicola was involved in a variety of activities in Philadel-

THOMAS MACHIN. *An extremely detailed map of the Hudson Highlands. Sparks Collection, Cornell University Library.*

phia. These may have included surveying, but his principal business was as a wholesale and retail merchant. He was an early member of the American Philosophical Society for which he wrote a paper on the preservation of biological specimens in alcohol, and he also edited "The American Magazine or General Repository" for a time.

Nicola was a whole-hearted supporter of the Revolution and during 1776 and 1777 published three military manuals. As early as July 1775, he proposed an "invalid" regiment for men with partial disabilities, and in June of 1777 was appointed Colonel of such a regiment. He was promoted to Brigadier in November 1783. Nicola is best remembered for his suggestion that Washington head a Royal American Government as Emperor. Following the Revolution Nicola moved to Alexandria, Virginia. He died August 4, 1807.

PLAN OF THE ENGLISH LINES NEAR PHILADELPHIA. 1777.
A carefully executed, detailed map of the part of the city along the Delaware and of the British line of fortifications north of the city extending from the Delaware, to the Schuylkill River. 14¾ x 38½. Plans and elevations of all the redoubts are given. Historical Society of Pennsylvania.

32. ISAAC NICOLL

Isaac Nicoll was born in New Windsor, N. Y. in 1741. He was a landowner and resident at the outbreak of the Revolution, an early member of the Committee of Safety and a militia officer. He served with the rank of Captain at Fort Constitution, across from New Windsor, in March 1776 and at Mount Washington in September 1776. His one known plan was made during this period. The so-called "Secret Committee" at Poughkeepsie appointed Nicoll one of the Commissioners of Sequestration on January 8, 1778.

It is interesting to note that the location of Nicoll's house is shown on DeWitt's map of the Windsor Cantonment of the American Army of 1783. Nicoll subsequently moved to Schralenburg, N. J., the present Bergenfield, where he died in 1804.

PLAN OF FORT PROPOSED ON THE EAST OF FORT CONSTITUTION.
On verso "received May 10th 1776" "laid down by Scale of 20 Feet to and inch" "Isaac Nicoll". Careful outline plan of a star shaped fort "From this Fort to the Blockhouse is 83 chanes and to the Gravel Hill 51 chanes". 12 x 13. Sparks Collection, Cornell University Library. MPI 522.

33. JOHN NORMAN

John Norman was born in England about 1748 and emigrated to Philadelphia by May 1774 as a self-styled "Architect and Landscape Engraver." He published a folio reprint of Abraham Swan's "British Architect" in 1775 and later, the "Collection of Designs in Architecture" by the same author. The first contained a monumental 60 folio plates. In 1776 in Philadelphia he engraved the "Plan of the town of Boston" for Murray's war history and also the portraits of American officers used in the same volume (Volume I). The latter were not as skilfully executed as the former, however.

In 1783 Norman moved to Boston and published a reprint of the "British Architect" and a compilation of his own entitled "Town and Country Builders Assistant." Other ventures were an edition of William Poin's "Practical Builder;" "The Boston Directory," in 1789 and the first published; and the "Boston Magazine" which included at intervals a "Geographical Gazetteer of Massachusetts." Norman died in Boston June 8, 1817 after a busy career and was buried on Copps Hill.

PLAN OF THE TOWN OF BOSTON WITH THE ATTACK ON BUNKER'S HILL, IN THE PENINSULA OF CHARLESTON, ON JUNE 17, 1775.
A carefully executed but not remarkable engraving 7 x 11½. Published in *An Impartial History of the present war in America* by Rev. James Murray, Boston 1781, Vol. 1, page 430.

34. THOMAS PALMER

Thomas Palmer appears first in a letter dated December 17, 1775 in which he, with Colonel Isaac Nicoll and Mr. Livingston were directed to forward cannon to the Committee of Safety. Later, he was appointed to superintend the construction of fortifications at Fort Montgomery, and was instructed to apply to General Charles Lee for an engineer to help. He forwarded a letter dated April 28, 1776 to Frederick Rhinelander, enclosing a map which predates the following map, the latter being designated as No. 2.

The New York State Library has a field and survey book of Palmer's which he had made prior to the Revolution.

A ROUGH MAP OF FORT MONTGOMERY SHOWING ITS SITUATION ON PUPLOPES POINT GROUND PLOT OF THE BUILDINGS ETC. ETC. PER T. P. NO. 2.
On verso "Plan of the Works at Fort Montgomery May 31, 1776 No. 2". A boldly drawn ms. 15¼ x 19. It bears a note in the hand of Jared Sparks "See Ld. Sterling's letter to Washington June 1, 1776". Sparks Collection, Cornell University Library.

> *Note*: A lithograph reproduction of a "Plan of Fort Montgomery, made late 1776 on occasion of visit by Lord Sterling drawn by Colonel Palmer 1776". 7¾ x 10. This is included in Vol. I opposite page 474 of the *Calender of Historical Manuscripts relating to the War of the Revolution*, published in Albany in 1868 by the Secretary of State of New York.
> One of the maps in Force's *American Archives,* the 4th series, has a plan following page 736. These five lithographed plans of the fortifications in the West Point-Fort Constitution area are reproduced on four pages. One "Sketch of a Map showing the present situation of the fortifications already erected and to be erected" is initialed "T.P.", probably Thomas Palmer.

35. JOSEPH PHILLIPS

Joseph Phillips was born near Maidenhead, now Lawrenceville, N. J., about 1718. In 1776 he was appointed a Major in the New Jersey Battalion, the first military organization in the state, and served in the Battle of Long Island. He was promoted to Lieutenant Colonel, and in 1777 to Colonel of the 1st Regiment of Hunterdon County, his regiment forming part of General Nathaniel Heard's Brigade.

Phillips continued to serve until August 1780. He died in 1788.

PLAN OF ROADS FROM TRENTON TO PRINCETON JANY 1777. COL. PHILLIPS.
A crude manuscript map 12 x 13¼ demonstrating extensive local knowledge. This was probably used by Major Henry Knox. Historical Society of Pennsylvania.

36. Elijah Porter

Elijah Porter was surveyor for Hartford County, Connecticut in the 1760's. He was one of the many local surveyors whose work was employed by or incorporated into Erskine's surveys. As noted previously, Erskine was scrupulous in giving credit. ERSKINE-DEWITT 40.
Course of Farmington River. This Survey of Farmington River was taken Anno Domine 1765 by Mr. Porter Surveyor of Farmington. Manuscript survey 15½ x 20¼. New York Historical Society.

37. Rufus Putnam

Rufus Putnam was born at Sutton, Massachusetts in 1738 and served in the Lake Champlain region during the French and Indian War. On May 19, 1775, he was appointed a Lieutenant Colonel in Brewer's Massachusetts Regiment. He subsequently transferred to the 2nd Continental Infantry on January 1, 1776 and on August 5, 1776 was promoted to Colonel of Engineers. On November 1, 1776 he transferred as a field officer to the 5th Massachusetts Regiment. He was promoted to Brigadier General in the Continental Army January 7, 1783 and served until 1792. During this period he was at Boston, New York, West Point, under Gates at Saratoga and with Wayne at Stony Point. Putnam was one of the many who built or rebuilt West Point's fortifications. What prompted the map of Narragansett Bay which is noted below is not evident.

After the Revolution, Putnam was an organizer of the Ohio Company of Volunteers in 1786 and together with Manassah Cutler, was one of the founders of Marietta, Ohio. In 1792 he was appointed to deal with the hostile Maumee Indians.

Putnam filled the post of U. S. Surveyor General from 1796 to 1803 but was severely handicapped by his deficiency in mathematics. He died May 1, 1824.
(1) A MAP OF THE NARRAGANSETT BAY IN THE COLONY OF RHODE ISLAND WITH THE SEVERAL ISLANDS & HARBOURS INCLUDED THEREIN ACCORDING TO THE LATEST DRAUGHTS WITH SEVERAL AMENDMENTS MADE ACCORDING TO OBSERVATIONS AND SURVEYS TAKEN BY LIEUT. COL. PUTNAM JANUARY 7TH, 1776 PRESENTED TO HIS EXCELLENCY GEORGE WASHINGTON ESQ.
A roughly done ms. 14½ x 19¼ showing little or nothing of military or geographical importance. Sparks Manuscripts, Harvard College Library.
(2) A PLAN OF THE BATTLES OF FREEMAN'S FARM AND BEMIS' HEIGHTS.
Published in Charles Wilson's *Account of the Burgoyne Campaign,* Albany 1844 from an original ms. which has been lost.

The forwarding letter from Putnam dated January 7, 1776 is preserved in the Washington Manuscripts in the Library of Congress.

38. David Pye

David Pye was one of those men whose local knowledge was incorporated into Erskine's great cartographic corpus but about whom little is known. He is referred to on the map noted below as "D^d Pye Esq." "Roads about Clarkstown &c." Pye was the proprietor of a mercantile establishment at Clarkstown in Orange County, New York, close to the New Jersey border.

He was chairman of a "Committee on the South Side of the Mountain" at the outbreak of the Revolution. He received a letter from General Wayne dated August 9, 1781 at Tappan relating to brass for military cap ornaments and the dyeing of red material for uniforms. Pye was a frequent representative for Orange County at the Provincial Congress of the state.
ROADS ABOUT CLARKSTOWN &C BY D^D PYE ESQ.
(missing).
(Number 27 of the Erskine-DeWitt series). New York Historical Society.

39. David Rittenhouse

David Rittenhouse was another source of cartographic data used by Erskine.

Rittenhouse was born in Germantown near Philadelphia in 1732. His early training as a clockmaker prepared him for his career as America's first distinguished astronomer and maker of precision and mathematical instruments. Using his own instruments, he surveyed the boundary between Pennsylvania and Delaware. In 1769 he observed the transit of Venus at the request of the American Philosophical Society of which he was a member.

Rittenhouse was active in public affairs as well as being an innovator in the instrument field. He served on the State Constitutional Convention Committee, as State Treasurer and, later, as Director of the U. S. Mint. He followed Franklin as President of the American Philosophical Society. Rittenhouse died in 1796.
THE RIVER SCHUYKILL FROM FALLS TO READING BY D^D RITTENHOUSE WITH THE DEPTHS A, B, D, A CONTRACTION OF D^O. (Map 89 of the Erskine-DeWitt series.)
(89A) A PLAN OF THE RIVER SCHUYLKILL WHEREIN ARE LAID DOWN THE SEVERAL SHOALS WITH THE DEPTH OF WATER AT EACH IN INCHES, ALSO THE DEPTH OF THE CHANNEL IN GENERAL IN THE BEGINNING OF AUGUST 1773. TOGETHER WITH THE MEANS PROPOSED FOR IMPROVING THE NAVIGATION OF S^D RIVER AND AN ESTIMATE OF THE EXPENSE. COPIED FROM THE ORIGINAL PLAN OF DAVID RITTENHOUSE ESQ^R BY ROBT. ERSKINE F.R.S. 1779.
(89B) (Inset section of the above on the same scale in the area of Norristown). Carefully executed ms. 14¾ x 147.

40. Etienne de Rochefontaine

Etienne Nicholas Marie Béchet de Rochefontaine was born February 23, 1755 at Aij, France. He was the son of a wine merchant but chose to become a military engineer. He began service in the American Army on March 13, 1778 when he was commissioned a Captain of Engineers. He was promoted to Major on November 16, 1781 and retired December 15, 1783.

Rochefontaine's service to France included a tour of duty as Adjutant General to Santo Domingo in 1791, from whence he came in 1792 as a refugee from the French Revolution to New York. He served as a temporary engineer from March 29, 1794 and worked on the fortification of New England. Rochefontaine was appointed Lieutenant Colonel of the 1st Regiment of Engineers on February 26, 1795 and served in this position until his retirement on May 7, 1798. He died in New York City January 30, 1814 and was buried at St. Paul's.

(1) (ENCAMPMENT AT MORRISTOWN).
A carefully executed ms. of Morristown and the adjacent area showing the American encampment, with border, 10 x 11¼. The legend is in the lower right corner with "by Cap^T Rochefontaine Eng^R" in the lower left. This map accompanied a letter from General Nathaniel Greene dated January 16, 1780 to Washington concerning the defensibility of Morristown against attack. Library of Congress.

(2) PLAN DE LA RECONNAISSANCE FAIT LE 21 JUILLET 81 PAR LES GENEREAUX WASHINGTON ET DE ROCHAMBEAU LA POSITION DES OUVRAGES ANGLAIS ET LES PRINCIPEAUX POINTS DU PLAN ON ETE DETERMINES GEOMETRIQUEMENT PAR M. DE ROCHEFONTAINE CAPT^E INGENIEUR ON SERVICE DES ESTATS UNIS.
A carefully finished manuscript survey of the British defenses of New York City. 40 x 41 cm. Number 304 in the Karpinski Collection from the original in the French Naval Archives.

The meeting between Washington and Rochambeau resulted in the decision to mount an attack upon the British in the south, eventually Yorktown, rather than an attack upon New York.

41. BERNARD ROMANS

Bernard Romans was born in the Netherlands about 1720 and was probably educated as an engineer in England. He was sent to America about 1757 and served as a surveyor in Georgia. Romans was appointed Deputy Surveyor of Georgia in 1766 and a short time later went to East Florida to survey the property of Lord Egmont, the associate of Oglethorpe in founding Georgia. Romans acquired property of his own in Florida.

The Surveyor-General for the Southern District, William Gerard deBrahm, promoted Romans to the post of principal Deputy Surveyor for the District. In 1773 Romans sold his Florida property, left his post and moved to New York City, with the probable plan of publishing his accounts of East Florida and charts of the Florida waters. The same year he was made a member of the New York Marine Society and of the American Philosophical Society; and a letter dated 1773 at Pensacola on an improved mariner's compass was published later in the American Philosophical Society Proceedings.

During the next few years Romans was in various New England cities. There is a record of a receipt signed by him for payment for a set of charts of the navigation to the southward of Georgia to Isaac Beers of New Haven.

In April 1775 Romans was appointed a member of a committee commissioned to take Fort Ticonderoga. He accompanied the expedition headed by Benedict Arnold but did not participate in the capture. Instead he independently captured nearby Fort George. Romans aided in the removal of the ordnance from Ticonderoga which was later moved to Boston under Henry Knox. Next he was recommended by Washington for appointment to report on construction of fortifications at Fort Constitution in 1775. His report to the Committee of Safety of New York was accompanied by a set of plans. The area was found to be commanded by the higher land of West Point across the Hudson River. This defect was studied by a congressional committee and resulted in Lord Stirling recommending the occupation and fortification of West Point.

On February 8, 1776 Romans was commissioned a Captain of the 1st Pennsylvania Company of Artillery. He was in "Sorrell" on May 15, 1776, a member of the retreating forces from the unsuccessful Quebec venture, when he wrote a letter relating to an appointment in his company. On July 24, 1776 a court of inquiry was convened under General Gates because

of a disagreement between Romans and a brother officer. Romans' military career ended by resignation June 1, 1778.

In the following year on January 28, Romans married Elizabeth Whitney of Weathersfield, Connecticut. A son Hubertus was born October 23. Later Romans joined the Southern Army and was captured in 1780, a short time after writing a character reference for Captain Thomas Machin to James Clinton.

Romans was a prisoner at Montego Bay, Jamaica. He was repatriated late in 1783 and died at sea in January 1784, possibly murdered.

(1) PLAN OF A PART OF HUDSON'S RIVER NEAR & ABOUT THE FORTIFICATIONS NOW ERECTING IN THE HIGHLANDS.
A finished plan of the Hudson from below Buttermilk Falls to south of New Windsor 12¼ x 14½. "Scale is four inches makes a mile". The right lower segment of the sheet has a detailed "description of the Works already finished & further to be finished at this post". All the fortifications are on Constitution Island and none yet at West Point. Signed in ornate script "B. Romans Engineer". United States Military Academy, West Point. M4022.

(2) (THE HUDSON RIVER)
From below Dunderberg (present Bear Mountain) to south of New Windsor. A careful, somewhat less detailed survey 18½ x 21. Note on lower left "places where the committee of the Cont^L Congress ordered me to make out an estimate for & where would make a Battery of 12 heavy cannon." United States Military Academy, West Point. M 4028.

> Note: Force's *American Archives,* the 4th series, on page 725 and following records a letter to the Committee of Safety of New York, dated September 14, 1775 at Marteleer's Rock, the site of Fort Constitution, from Bernard Romans. The letter forwards five plans of intended fortifications in the Highlands. The plans and letter are quite detailed in respect to armament, places for a potential enemy landing and ends by saying "this is the most frugal plan that can be of any service here." The five lithographed plans on four pages are concerned only with Fort Constitution. Two of these may have been based upon the foregoing plans. One of these, "sketch of a Map showing the present situation of the Fortifications already Erected and to be erected" is initialed "T.P.", probably Thomas Palmer.

(3) TO THE HON^L JN^O HANCOCK ESQ^{RE} PRESIDENT OF YE CONTINENTAL CONGRESS THIS MAP OF THE SEAT OF CIVIL WAR IN AMERICA IS RESPECTFULLY INSCRIBED BY HIS MOST OBEDIENT SERVANT B. ROMANS.
16 x 17. An engraved map with inset "Plan of Boston and its Environs 1775" and another inset "A View of the Lines thrown up upon Boston Neck by the Ministerial Army". Among the references noted is the location of Mr. Hancock's house. The map was printed by James Rivington in New York in August 1775. It appears in two states, the second having a legend along the right border "Post Roads, Roads Not Post Roads, County Lines, Township Lines, Province Lines".
The map was advertised for sale at 5 shillings when printed in Rivington's *New-York Gazette* August 3, 1775. The August 31, 1775 issue of the same journal indicated "Romans Boston Map is just printed, will in a few days be published and sold by James Rivington, and Messrs Noel and Hazard".

(4) A GENERAL MAP OF THE SOUTHERN BRITISH COLONIES, IN AMERICA COMPREHENDING NORTH AND SOUTH CAROLINA, GEORGIA, EAST AND WEST FLORIDA, WITH THE NEIGHBORING INDIAN COUNTRIES. FROM THE MODERN SURVEYS OF ENGINEER DEBRAHM, CAPT. COLLET, MOUZON & OTHERS AND FROM THE LARGE HYDROGRAPHICAL SURVEY OF THE COASTS OF EAST AND WEST FLORIDA. BY B. ROMANS, 1776. LONDON. PRINTED FOR R. SAYER AND J. BENNETT, MAP, CHART AND PRINTSELLERS NO. 53 FLEET STREET, AS THE ACT DIRECTS, 15TH OCTBR. 1776.

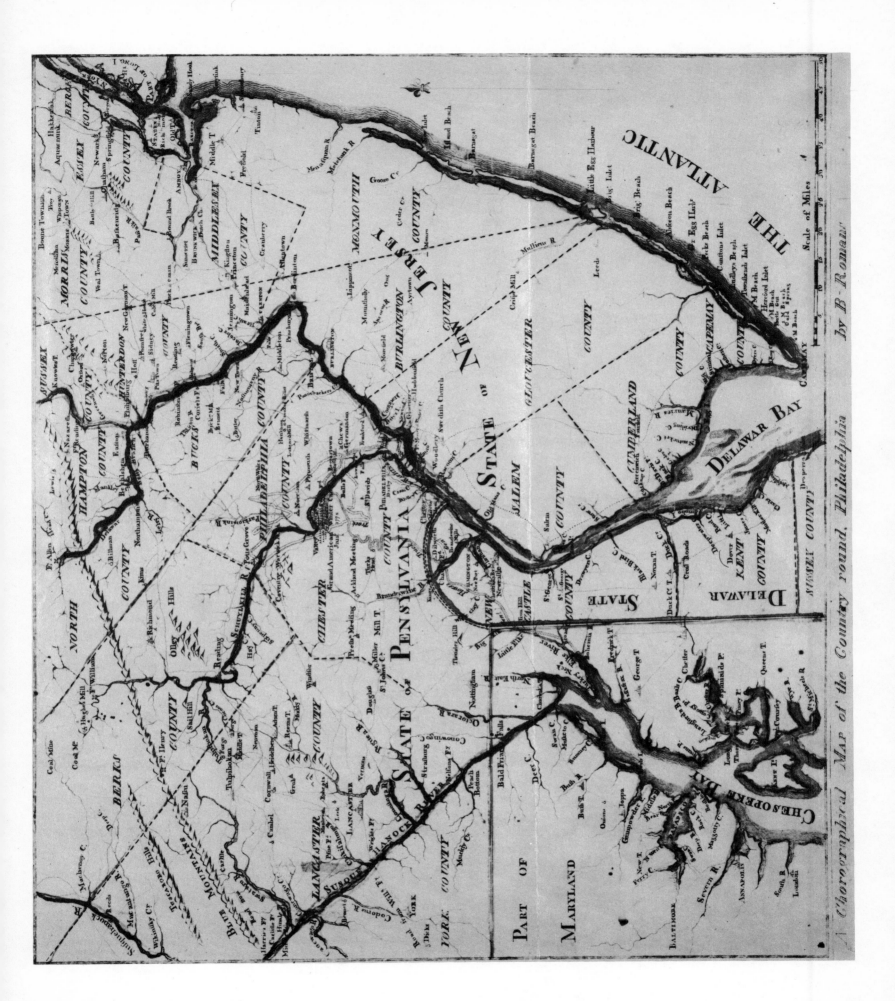

BERNARD ROMANS. *A printed map showing military operations through early 1778.* John Carter Brown Library.

31

A good contemporary printed map 19 x 24¼. It was a compilation made by the firm of Sayer and Bennett, one of England's two competing map publishers, semi-official printers of military maps. The map includes an inset plan of Charlestown and St. Augustine. It was No. 5 of six folding maps in "The American Military Pocket Atlas". This was also known as the "Holster Atlas" owing to its small 8 vo. size, made for use of mounted officers. Romans was the only American to have his map published and used by the enemy.

(5) CONNECTICUT AND PARTS ADJACENT.
An unsigned, undated, engraved map 20½ x 23¾. A scale of miles at bottom. The map shows roads in great detail in some areas but not others. Among the points identified are Murderers Kill or Murders Kills, the first time so identified. Beverly Robinson's, Fort Constitution and Verplanks Point are identified but Stony Point is not shown. A proposal for the printing of this map was dated at New Haven, April 21, 1777 and published in the "Boston Gazette and Country Journal" May 19, 1777. Another dated New Haven, June 11, 1777 and published in the "Connecticut Journal" of the same day indicates that the map had just been published and was for sale by Messrs. Elias Beers and Zina Dennison of New Haven. It notes that "the whole is the Manufacture of this town." The "Connecticut Gazette" and the "Universal Intelligencer" of October 31, 1777 advertise the map had just been published and was for sale by T. Green. Charles Evans' "American Bibliography", Vol 5, page 348 notes "Just published and to be sold by Nathaniel Townsend, in Norwich". Copies of this rare map are in the John Carter Brown and Huntington Libraries and the Mellon Collection.

(6) CONNECTICUT AND PARTS ADJACENT.
H. Klockhoff, sculp. An engraved map 20⅝ x 23¼ published in Amsterdam by Covens and Mortier, 1780, and nearly identical with the previous. Dated at New Haven and the finished map advertised for sale in the "New London Gazette", June 5, 1778. The only copy formerly owned by Henry N. Stevens of London.
Library of Congress.

(7) A CHOROGRAPHICAL MAP OF THE COUNTRY ROUND PHILADELPHIA BY B. ROMANS.
An engraved map 11½ x 13 of almost all of New Jersey, Delaware, North Eastern Maryland and South Eastern Pennsylvania. Among the points of interest are "Grand American Winter Camp 1778" at Valley Forge, "Howes' Track" and "Genᴸ Washington's Track" somewhat inaccurately shown. The map was advertised as "Just published at New Haven" in the "Connecticut Courant" of June 2, 1778. John Carter Brown Library.

(8) A CHOROGRAPHICAL MAP OF THE COUNTRY ROUND PHILADELPHIA.
Engraved map 12½ x 13 published at Amsterdam by Covens and Mortier and Covens junior probably 1780. Engraved by H. Klockhoff. Library of Congress.

42. ALEXANDER SCAMMELL

Alexander Scammell was the son of a physician. Born March 27, 1747 at Mendon (now Milford) Massachusetts, he graduated from Harvard in 1769 and taught school at Kingston and later at Plymouth, Massachusetts. In 1772 he went to Plymouth, New Hampshire to aid the Royal Navy in surveying timberlands. Here he was associated with Samuel Holland, an accomplished surveyor and Surveyor General of the Northern District. Holland's map of New York, New Jersey and part of Pennsylvania was later published by Sayer and Bennett and was widely used by both sides during the Revolution. Scammell himself submitted a map of Maine's pine forests in 1772. Subsequently, Scammell began to read law with John Sullivan, later General Sullivan, at Durham, New Hampshire.

The outbreak of the Revolution interrupted Scammell's studies. He joined the military with an appointment as Brigade Major, and served under Sullivan in the siege of Boston and the expedition to Canada. In the Long Island campaign when he was aide to Sullivan he made a blunder fortunately recouped by Washington. Scammell was made Brigade Major in the division of General Charles Lee in October 1776 and later, on December 10, 1776, Colonel of the 3rd Continental Battalion which had been raised by New Hampshire. He served with General St. Clair at Ticonderoga and was slightly wounded at Saratoga.

Scammell, as the choice of Congress, succeeded Timothy Pickering as Adjutant General. In this capacity, he arrested his former commander Charles Lee after the Battle of Monmouth and was in charge of John Andre's execution in 1780.

Scammell wearied of the responsibility as Adjutant General and resigned to take command of the 1st New Hampshire Regiment. He led a party of Continental light horse until September 30, 1781 when he was captured at Yorktown while leading a scouting expedition. He died of his wounds on October 6, 1781 at Williamsburg.

(NEW YORK CITY AND VICINITY) TO THE HONORᴸᴱ JOHN SULLIVAN ESQᴿ MAJOR GEN'L IN THE ARMY OF THE UNITED STATES OF AMERICA HUMBLY PRESENTED BY HIS OBEDT. SERT. ALEX. SCAMMELL.
An accurate but roughly done ms. 12¾ x 15½ of Manhattan Island and adjacent New Jersey, Westchester and Long Island. There is a key to various locations and a scale of miles. American Antiquarian Society.

43. WILLIAM SCULL

William Scull was raised in the household of his grandfather Nicholas, Surveyor General of Pennsylvania. In 1770 he published a map of the Province of Pennsylvania which was engraved by Henry Dawkins and printed by James Nevil in Philadelphia. This was largely a compilation of the work of other surveyors and was republished in many editions in France and England.

On September 30, 1776 Scull was commissioned a Captain in the 11th Pennsylvania Regiment but retired on July 1, 1778 to join the Geographer's Department under Erskine. He served until late the following year. His name does not appear on any map after No. 99.

Scull was recorded as a member of the American Philosophical Society from Reading, Pa.

(1) SURVEY IN N. Y. & CONN. STATES, FOR HIS EXCELLENCY GEN. WASHINGTON, BY ROBERT ERSKINE F.R.S. ANNO 1778 W. SCULL DELIN.
A carefully executed ms. 16¼ x 31 covering from Bedford, N.Y. north to Dover and east to Danbury, Conn. A gift to the New York Historical Society in 1845 from Thomas Gordon of Trenton, publisher of a gazetteer and map of New Jersey. New York Historical Society. J-2.

(2) SURVEYS IN NEW YORK AND CONNECTICUT STATES, FOR HIS EXCELLENCY GEN. WASHINGTON, BY ROBERT ERSKINE, F.R.S. ANNO 1778 W. SCULL, DELIN.
A carefully done ms. 15¾ x 31 which includes the Hudson River from "Newborough" to lower Haverstraw Bay. It is the left hand portion of the previous map. Also a gift of Thomas Gordon. New York Historical Society. J-3.

(3) ROAD FROM QUIBBLETOWN TO AMBOY & PLACES BY BEARINGS PR CAPT. SCULL.
Manuscript survey 13½ x 26 typical of the other Erskine-DeWitt series. New York Historical Society (Erskine-DeWitt No. 55).

(4) CONTRACTION IN THE JERSEYS 2 MILES TO AN INCH, A, B, C.

By Order of the Honorable Continental Congress. the Fort which this is the Plan of
was laid out. Feb 1776. at Pooploperis Kiln in the Highlands
of New York and Nam'd after the brave Gen Mongomery
Wm Smith Engineer

Explanation
A A A A Platforms for Cannon
B B B Barracks
C Magazine
D Blind to the Entering Port
C C C C C C C C Works to be finish'd first
32, 32 Where the Heavy Cannon are to be plac'd

A Scale of 50 Paces   3 ft to a pace

the Plan of the Profile

WILLIAM SMITH. "A plan of Fort Montgomery", near the present Bear Mountain. Massachusetts Historical Society.

Large Paper by Capt. Scull. New York Historical Society (Erskine-DeWitt No. 98).

A. *Contraction in the Jerseys.* A ms. 17½ x 29½ on a conical projection covering Reddington, Amboy and Pompton.

B. *Contraction in the Jerseys.* As above 19½ x 29½ covering New Brunswick, Pluckemin and Springfield.

C. *Contraction in the Jerseys.* As above 19 x 28½. Pompton Northwest and Southwest.

(5) Projections of Lat. & Departure for Closing & Trying the Meeting of Surveys. (2 miles to an inch). (Erskine-DeWitt No. 99).

A. *General Contraction of the Road from near Chester in New Jersey to Chestnut Hill in Pennsylvania For the purpose of projecting and adjusting the different surveys into a general map. Scale 2 miles to an inch.* A carefully drawn but incomplete ms. 21¼ x 29¼.

B. *Projection &c for closing and trying the meeting of Surveys — 2 miles an inch.* As above 21 x 29½ locating New Brunswick, Easton, Bethlehem, Allentown and Trenton, etc.

C. *Projections &c for closing and trying the meeting of Surveys. 2 miles an inch.* As above 18 x 29½ locating Mount Holly, Crosswicks, Bristol and Philadelphia, etc.

D. *Projections for Closing and trying the meeting of the Surveys, 2 miles to an inch.* As above 19¾ x 28 locating White Plains, Fishkill, Warwick, etc.

44. William Smith

William Smith was appointed a Captain and served as an engineer to relieve and succeed Bernard Romans in February 1776. He surveyed and staked out an intended fortification which became Fort Montgomery. He was succeeded by Thomas Machin.

(Plan of Fort Montgomery) By Order of the Honerable (sic) Continental Congress the Fort Which This is the Plan of was Laid Out Feb. 1776 at Vooplopens Kiln (sic) in the Highlands of New-York and Named After the Brave Genl Montgomery. Wm. Smith Engineer.

A careful plan of the fort as originally designed 11½ x 16¼ with the explanation in the lower left. There is a plan of the profile of the works at bottom center. Massachusetts Historical Society.

45. Griffin Spencer

Griffin Spencer characterized himself as "lover of learning & ingeneous arts" when he signed his crude map of the siege of Yorktown. Spencer, of East Greenwich, Rhode Island, served as a private in the Rhode Island Regiment probably under Captain Stephen Olney.

(Siege of Yorktown) This Place is What the Enemy Had Possession of Within These lines is the Compact Part of Little York in Virginia.

A very crude and rough sketch plan 13 x 16¼. Yale University Library *783 nc/Y 82/1781G.

46. John Trumbull

John Trumbull was born in Lebanon, Connecticut in 1756, son of the Colonial Governor Jonathan Trumbull. He graduated from Harvard in 1773.

With the onset of the Revolution, Trumbull served as Aide to General Joseph Spencer who had proceeded to Jamaica Plain close to Boston with his Connecticut regiment. He then served as an Aide to Washington and finally to General Gates, by that time having achieved the rank of Colonel. Trumbull resigned his commission in 1777. The map of Boston Neck was made during his first duty and that of Ticonderoga just before his resignation.

Trumbull studied art in Boston in 1778 and, after a brief stint as Aide to General John Sullivan on Rhode Island, went to London in 1780 to study in the studio of Benjamin West. During the John Andre affair he was imprisoned for a short time reprisal. His military experience definitely influenced his choice of subject. During the period between the cessation of hostilities and Trumbull's return to America in 1792, he completed many paintings with an American military theme at West's studio in London, among them his "Battle of Bunker's Hill" and "Death of Montgomery." He was a member of the American Philosophical Society.

Trumbull continued to paint in America, designed several buildings and executed the paintings in the rotunda of the Capitol. He died in 1841 in New York City.

(1) General Sketch of the Lines at Charleston Prospect Hill & Roxbury.

An accurate but rough manuscript sketch which was forwarded to Congress by General Washington in a letter August 4, 1775. There is a key of 23 descriptive points on the left side of the map headed by "Explanation". Library of Congress.

(2) Boston & the Surrounding Country & Posts of the American Troops.

Folding engraved map 7 x 10¾ in borders, based upon the preceding. In Trumbull's *Autobiography,* New York 1841.

(3) (British Lines on Boston Neck).

A detailed, carefully drawn manuscript plan of the British fortifications defending Boston Neck. 12¾ x 14¾. There is a notation that details of armament were obtained from a deserter from the Welsh Fusileers. The plan has a detailed table of the armaments keyed to numbered locations made by Thomas Mifflin, Washington's Aide. American Philosophical Society.

Note: Trumbull made the above by crawling close to the British works. The accuracy of the sketches was confirmed by a deserter. Trumbull considered this the reason for his rapid promotion as the sketches were completed by the time of Washington's arrival after his appointment as Commander-in-Chief by Congress.

(4) (New London Harbor).

Careful manuscript sketch 7¾ x 12¾ indicating lines of fire from four fortifications. April 1776. Connecticut State Library.

(5) (Ticonderoga).

A manuscript map 8 x 8½ in a letter. Shows title of Ticonderoga but shows "A Encampment" on the opposite shore. Mount Defiance is shown as "Inacesible Nik". Company places and Infantry points indicated. Connecticut State Library.

(6) Ticonderoga & Its Dependencies August 1777 J. T.

Engraved map 8½ x 11 based upon the preceding but in greater detail. In Trumbull's *Autobiography,* New York 1841.

47. Jean de Villefranche

Jean Louis Ambroise de Genton, Chevalier de Villefranche was born December 9, 1747 at Albi in the south of France. He was trained as a military engineer and became a 2nd Lieutenant June 1, 1772 and a 1st Lieutenant July 1, 1773. In February 1777 he came to America with Tronson du Coudray.

Villefranche was appointed Captain of Engineers August 12, 1777, promoted to Major on January 1, 1778 and brevetted Lieutenant Colonel on May 2, 1783. His first duties were in

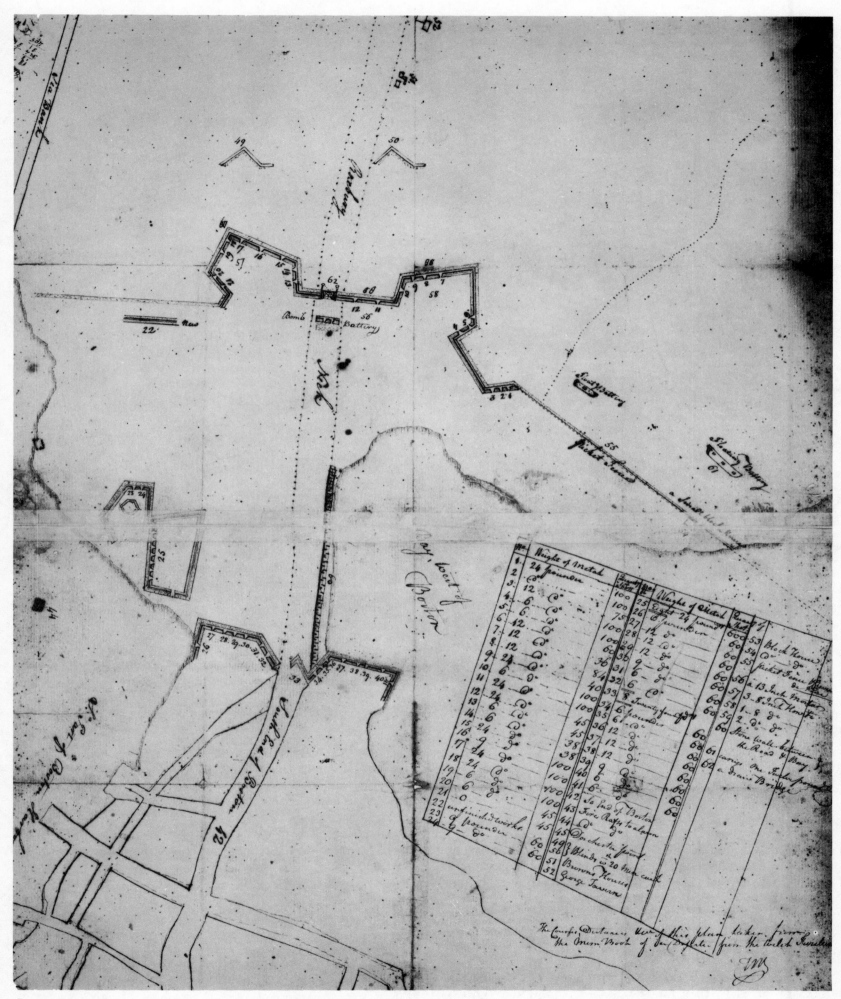

JOHN TRUMBULL. *British fortifications on Boston Neck. Table was probably by Thomas Mifflin. American Philosophical Society.*

the fortification of the Delaware in 1777 and his later duties were with the development of fortifications at West Point and adjacent areas in the Hudson Highlands.

(1) (FORTS ON THE DELAWARE).
Carefully executed, detailed ms. of both shores of the Delaware River including part of Philadelphia and extending southward to below Hog Island. Fortifications, roads, property lines, channels and obstructions to navigation in detail. The irregularly shaped sheet is 51¼ x 61¼ overall. There are overlays on Mud Island and Philadelphia indicating proposed changes. A tracing is in the Historical Society of Pennsylvania, the original being in the Bureau of Land Reclamation, Harrisburg, Pa.

(2) (REDOUBTS ON CARPENTER'S AND PROVINCE ISLANDS)
A highly finished, detailed plan with profiles of the works. 10¼ x 15 with a border. These redoubts were built on the two islands which lay south of the mouth of the Schuylkill River between Mud Island and the Pennsylvania Mainland. Not signed by Villefranche but countersigned below border by Duportail. Library of Congress.

(3) (POWDER MAGAZINE).
A careful manuscript plan 8¾ x 14½ with a description of construction under "Observations". These indicate that the magazine is to be built on an island and can not be dug into the earth. Signed in lower right corner "Villefranche eng^{ER}" and countersigned below border by Duportail. Library of Congress.

(4) (MAP OF WEST POINT).
A detailed finished copy of the original. 22 x 31. The original was found in Washington's papers and presented to the U. S. Military Academy in 1852. It has since disappeared but a facsimile is preserved. It shows Fort Arnold close to the River and Fort Putnam further away on a higher elevation. A Battery and Forts 5, 6 and 7 are seen on Constitution Island.

(5) (THE HUDSON RIVER).
A carefully finished manuscript map of the Hudson from north of West Point to south of Stony Point. 14 x 18¾. The map has previously been folded and has construction lines in pencil, the remainder in ink. It is nearly identical with that published in Boynton's "History of West Point". Scale is 1 foot to the mile. Signed at top "Villefranche Maj eng^R". Private Collection.

48. ISAAC VROOMAN

Isaac Vrooman was one of a team of brothers who surveyed along the Mohawk River, along the Battenkill and in Albany County, New York. This was the "Vromer" referred to by Erskine in listing Map 88. In a letter to Washington dated March 20, 1779, Erskine reported that a surveyor had been hired to map Albany County. It is not known if the map was ever completed or delivered.

ERSKINE-DEWITT 88. THE COUNTY OF ALBANY BY MR. VROMER & A CONTRACTION OF D^O, A & B.
(missing).

49. GEORGE WASHINGTON

George Washington needs no biography. It is sufficient to emphasize his abilities and background as an accomplished and experienced surveyor. He was the maker of two maps falling within the scope of this study. He was a member of the American Philosophical Society.

(1) (MAP OF BOSTON AND CAMBRIDGE).
A rough sketch map made about 1775. It indicates the fortified areas. Library of Congress.

(2) THE FOLLOWING MAP OF THE CAYUGA, OR TEOGA BRANCH OF THE SUSQUEHANNA, IS LAID DOWN BY QUESS FROM AN ACCT. IN B^D GENL. HANDS LETTER OF THE 31ST

MARCH 1779 AS GIVEN TO HIM BY AN OLD - - - OF - - - COUNTY IN PENNS^A WHO FORMERLY LIVED AT CHEMUNG-BUT HAD NOT BEEN IN THE COUNTRY FOR 23 YEARS.
A rough but quite accurate sketch map which is surprisingly correct considering the data on which it was based. Library of Congress.

50. JOHN WATKINS

John Watkins was commissioned a 2nd Lieutenant in the 1st New York Regiment and served from February 24, 1776 to November of the same year. He was a Captain in Malcolm's Continental Regiment from March 11 to October 12, 1777 and then served with the Geographer's department under Erskine. A letter from General Wayne while at Totowa dated November 23, 1780 indicates that Watkins had requested aid.

After the Revolution, Watkins, who had always previously referred to himself as "Capt. William Watkins AB" entered law practice in New York City and remained in practice until after 1796.

(1) R(OAD) FROM 15 M. STONE NEAR SUFFRANS TO FT. LEE, HACKENSACK, CLOSTER, TAPPAN, CLARKSTOWN, HAVERSTRAW &C BY CAPT. JOHN W. WATKINS, A. B.
New York Historical Society. (Erskine-DeWitt Map No. 26.)
Part 1. A careful manuscript plan. 17½ x 24¾.
Part 2. Same. 18½ x 24.
Part 3. Same. 16½ x 24.

(2) PLAN CHARLESTOWN S. CAROLINA BY J. WATKINS.
Carefully drawn ms. 6¾ x 10 in border "by J. Watkins the angles taken by a small pocket compass". New York Historical Society. (Erskine-DeWitt Map No. 61.)

(3) PART OF THE COUNTIES OF BERGEN & ORANGE.
FROM A SURVEY MADE BY J^N. WATKINS. Carefully drawn ms. 5½ x 11¼ in borders. Shows west shore of the Hudson River from Fort Lee to Haverstraw and west to Belle Grove. Washington Papers, Library of Congress (44, 15).

(4) (FORTIFICATION ON SADDLE RIVER, N. J.).
Carefully drawn manuscript sketch of an irregularly shaped earthwork with border 5 x 5¾. The work overlooks Saddle River and shows roads to Pompton and Haverstraw. There is an accompanying description of the works and buildings employed. There is no record of construction of this fortification. The sketch was made and forwarded to General Anthony Wayne in a letter dated November 10, 1780 to demonstrate the abilities of the author, as a possible successor to Robert Erskine. Library of Congress.

51. ANONYMOUS MAPS

Selecting maps in this category has presented obvious difficulties. As noted previously, printed or signed maps present no problem, nor may attribution in the case of maps whose history is known be too difficult. However, in relatively recent years, many maps have appeared suddenly in archives without antecedent history.

The maps in this section have been arranged geographically.

(A) NEW ENGLAND

(1) AN IDEAL PLAN OF THE RIVER PENOBSCOT, MAGABADUCE &C&C SHEWING THE SITUATION OF GEN. LOVEL'S ARMY; THE AMERICAN FLEET, TRANSPORTS &C&C WITH THOSE OF THE ENEMY'S. AUGUST 6TH 1779.
10½ x 15½. Very carefully executed and finished ms., the general format and appearance of which is reminiscent of early 18th century English maps. There is an inset in the upper right, of the surround-

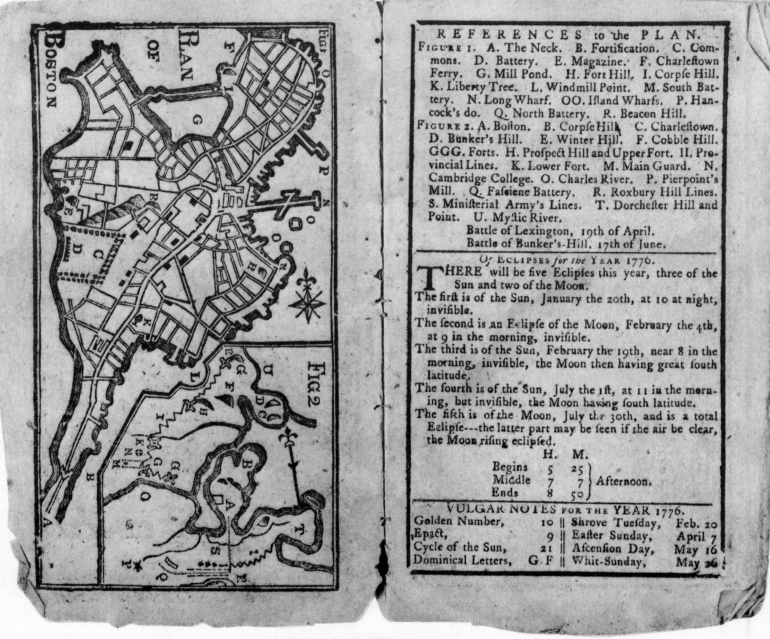

REFERENCES to the PLAN.

FIGURE 1. A. The Neck. B. Fortification. C. Commons. D. Battery. E. Magazine. F. Charlestown Ferry. G. Mill Pond. H. Fort Hill. I. Corpse Hill. K. Liberty Tree. L. Windmill Point. M. South Battery. N. Long Wharf. OO. Island Wharfs. P. Hancock's do. Q. North Battery. R. Beacon Hill.

FIGURE 2. A. Boston. B. Corpse Hill. C. Charlestown. D. Bunker's Hill. E. Winter Hill. F. Cobble Hill. GGG. Forts. H. Prospect Hill and Upper Fort. II. Provincial Lines. K. Lower Fort. M. Main Guard. N. Cambridge College. O. Charles River. P. Pierpoint's Mill. Q. Fascine Battery. R. Roxbury Hill Lines. S. Ministerial Army's Lines. T. Dorchester Hill and Point. U. Mystic River.

Battle of Lexington, 19th of April.
Battle of Bunker's-Hill, 17th of June.

Of ECLIPSES for the YEAR 1776.

THERE will be five Eclipses this year, three of the Sun and two of the Moon.

The first is of the Sun, January the 20th, at 10 at night, invisible.

The second is an Eclipse of the Moon, February the 4th, at 9 in the morning, invisible.

The third is of the Sun, February the 19th, near 8 in the morning, invisible, the Moon then having great south latitude.

The fourth is of the Sun, July the 1st, at 11 in the morning, but invisible, the Moon having south latitude.

The fifth is of the Moon, July the 30th, and is a total Eclipse---the latter part may be seen if the air be clear, the Moon rising eclipsed.

	H.	M.	
Begins	5	25	
Middle	7	7	Afternoon.
Ends	8	50	

VULGAR NOTES FOR THE YEAR 1776.

Golden Number,	10	Shrove Tuesday,	Feb. 20
Epact,	9	Easter Sunday,	April 7
Cycle of the Sun,	21	Ascension Day,	May 16
Dominical Letters,	G F	Whit-Sunday,	May 26

Among the first published war maps were those in the Almanacs. They were widely distributed; and most households purchased them before any other printed organ. The publishers were highly competitive and if they were not free plagarizers, at least used the same sources at the same time. Note the strong similarity between the maps of the New York area in the North American and Nathaniel Low cuts. "Bickerstaff's New-England Almanack for 1776", above. Isaac Warren's "North American Almanack for 1777", far left. "Nathaniel Low's Astronomical Diary for 1777", or almanac, at left. Sinclair Hamilton Collection, Princeton University Library.

ing area, in a gourd shaped border. There is a table of references outlining the whole operation in detail. Huntington Library, HM DE83.

(2) (PLAN OF BOSTON).
In "Hutchin's Improved; being an almanack and ephemeris 1776" published in New York by Hugh Gaine. The crude woodcut plan, 3½ x 6, is faced on the opposite leaf by "References to the plan". Library of Congress.

(3) (BOSTON AND ENVIRONS).
On verso of title page of "Bickerstaff's New-England Almanack. For the Year of Our Lord, 1776", printed by Robertsons and Trumbull. A woodcut plan of Boston showing the fortifications, magazine, Beacon Hill etc. and a smaller cut showing environs of Boston. The almanac, by Benjamin West, has a recipe for making gunpowder adapted for home use. Sinclair Hamilton Collection, Princeton University Library.

(4) A DRAUGHT OF THE HARBOUR OF BOSTON AND THE ADJACENT TOWNS & ROADS, 1775.
Title in rough cartouche. A rough manuscript road map 8½ x 12. Massachusetts Historical Society.

(5) A PLAN OF THE LINES ON WINTER HILL IN CHARLESTOWN JULY 5TH 1775.
Carefully executed ms. 13 x 16½. Sparks Manuscripts, Harvard University Library. PF 158.

(6) PLAN OF RHODE ISLAND THE DIFFERENT OPERATIONS OF THE FRENCH FLEET AND THE AMERICAN TROOPS UNDER MAJOR GENERAL SULLIVAN'S COMMAND; AGAINST THE LAND AND SEA BRITISH FORCES, SINCE THE 19TH AUGUST 1778 TO THE 30TH OF THE SAME MONTH AT NIGHT; WHEN THE AMERICANS RETREATED.
Accurate, carefully executed ms. 14½ x 30. The general appearance and format are reminiscent of the French map makers. This is supported by labeling the column of references at the left "Renvoy". Sparks Manuscripts, Harvard University Library. PF 158.

(B) NEW YORK

(1) (PLAN OF FORT TICONDEROGA AND SURROUNDING AREA).
Plan published in "Proceedings of a General Court Martial Held at White Plains in the State of New York by order of his Excellency General Washington Commander in Chief of the Army of the United States of America for the Trial of Major General St. Clair August 25, 1778, Major General Lincoln President. Philadelphia: Printed by Holland Sellers. MDCCLXXVIII." A carefully detailed engraved plan 9¾ x 12 with scale of miles. Newberry Library.

(2) (MAP OF THE EXPEDITION OF THE ARMY UNDER GENERAL JOHN SULLIVAN AGAINST THE INDIANS OF WEST NEW YORK IN THE SENECA & CAYUGA LAKE REGIONS, JUNE 18TH TO SEPTEMBER 15, 1779).
A carefully executed manuscript survey 27¾ x 28¼ of the entire route from its start at Easton, Pennsylvania. The encampments, local names and daily route are shown. Library of Congress.

(3) SKETCH OF HUDSON'S RIVER & SOUNDINGS NEAR POLOPAN ISLAND.
Careful but not finished ms. 13 x 15¼. Sparks Manuscripts, Harvard University Library. PF 158.

(4) (WEST POINT AND CONSTITUTION ISLAND).
Detailed careful ms. 13½ x 15. Scale in feet and miles. In references, Ft. Clinton (formerly Ft. Arnold). United States Military Academy. Map 3367.

(5) (CONSTITUTION ISLAND).
Carefully finished ink and wash drawing 14½ x 18¼ with borders. References to 5 batteries and their guns. On verso. "No. 3," apparently incomplete. Sparks Collection, Cornell University Library. MPI 523.

(6) (CONSTITUTION ISLAND).
Carefully executed ink and wash drawing in a border. 14½ x 19 by same hand as the preceding. The area is shown on a smaller scale from Constitution Island south to Stony Point. There is an inset elevation of the Highlands with a building. Appears incomplete. Marked "No. 1" on both sides. Sparks Collection, Cornell University Library. MPI 524.

(7) (FORT CONSTITUTION).
Elevation of river bank and fortifications. A careful ms. 8½ x 14 by the same hand as 523 and 524. Also incomplete. Sparks Collection, Cornell University Library. MPI 527b.

(8) MAP OF STONE POINT, VERPLANKS PT. ETC.
Rough ms. 13¼ x 16½. On verso, "from Genl Heath letter 3rd July 1779", labeled by George Washington. Sparks Collection, Cornell University Library. MPI 549.

(9) PLAN OF THE CAMP AND MANOUVERS OF THE ARMY AT VERPLANKS POINT.
Very carefully drawn and executed manuscript plan with borders. 11 x 20. Sparks Manuscripts, Harvard University Library. PF 158.

(10) PLAN OF THE CAMP ON VERPLANK'S POINT.
Carefully executed plan 8¼ x 17¼ by same hand as preceding. Sparks Manuscripts, Harvard University Library. PF 158.

(11) (NEW YORK ENVIRONS).
A rough woodcut map of New York Island and the adjacent areas in Isaac Warren's "The North American's Almanack, for the year of Our Lord Christ 1777, Worcester printed and sold by W. Stearns and D. Bigelow, also to be sold by the author in Lancaster". Sinclair Hamilton Collection, Princeton University Library.

(12) (MANHATTAN ISLAND AND ADJACENT AREAS).
Including lower Westchester County, Western Long Island, Staten Island and New Jersey in part. A detailed ms. 13¼ x 15¼ showing most of the movements of the New York campaign. This may have been made by Charles Wilson Peale. American Philosophical Society Library.

(13) PLAN OF THE REDOUBTS NEAR PHILIPSE 1 APRIL 1778, ON VERSO. STATE OF THE BRITISH LINES AND COUNTRY ON THE NORTH APRIL 1, 1778.
Manuscript plan 13½ x 17½. Manuscript Collection, New York Public Library.

(14) PLAN OF YORK ISLAND AND NEW JERSEY—INCORRECT.
On verso, "taken in 1776". Carefully drawn ms. on scale 2 miles - 1 inch. No border, references, fort at Red Hook, Point Battery, Fort Washington. 17 x 20. Historical Society of Pennsylvania. AM 602, 27.

(BB) SPY MAPS

The following maps of New York City and adjacent areas merit a prefatory note. In the later years of the War, a spy network was developed in the New York and Long Island area, directed toward regaining control from the British occupation forces. The quite sophisticated network used pseudonyms, code numbers, well developed "cover" and was directed by a "spy master", Benjamin Tallmadge. Tallmadge had a natural talent, excellent local knowledge and personal contacts, having been born and raised in Brookhaven, Long Island. Although many of the maps were enclosed in regular correspondence, it is difficult to determine the actual authorship. The more active spies and possible map makers were Abraham Bancker ("Amicus Republicae"), Louis Johnson Costigan ("Z"), Abraham Woodhull ("Samuel Culper" or "722" or "C"), Robert Townsend ("Samuel Culper Jr." or "723"), Austin Roe ("724"), John Hendricks ("John Hks." or "Mrs. Elizabeth Vanderhovon"), John and Joshua Mercereau, and John Vanderhoven ("D" or "L.D."). Tallmadge, incidentally, was "John Bolton", and the secret service or spy system was

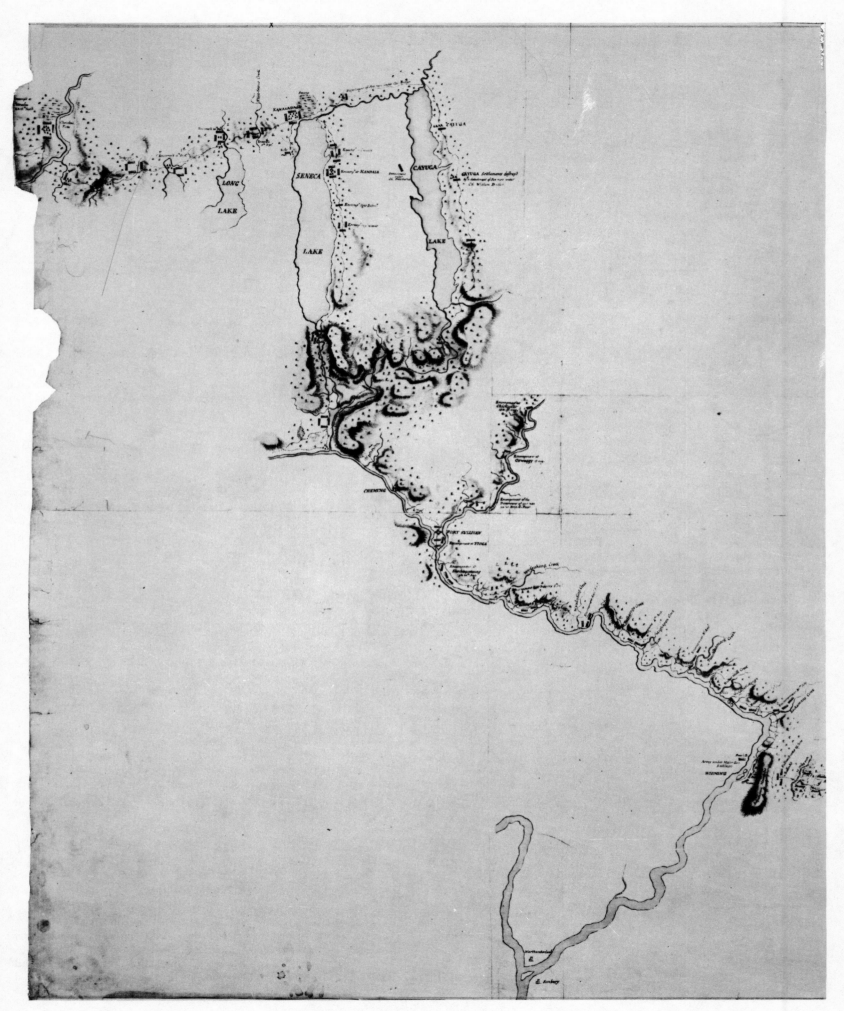

General John Sullivan's expedition against the Five Nations of the Iroquois in Western New York. Library of Congress.

"S.G.", which also served as a pseudonym for Tallmadge.

(1) (PLAN OF DEFENCES AT KINGSBRIDGE).
Crude, largely diagrammatic manuscript sketch of fortifications at the northern end of Manhattan Island and lower Bronx. 11¾ x 14¾. November 25, 1782. Library of Congress. Washington Papers (60, 157).

(2) (MANHATTAN AND BROOKLYN FORTIFICATIONS).
Crude, largely diagrammatic manuscript sketch of fortifications of lower Manhattan and Brooklyn. 4½ x 7½. November 6, 1780. Library of Congress. Washington Papers (Vol. 156 p. 20941).

(3) (MANHATTAN FORTIFICATIONS).
Crude, largely diagrammatic manuscript sketch of fortifications in lower Manhattan. 8¼ x 13. July 26, 1780. Library of Congress. Washington Papers (Vol. 143 p. 19104).

(4) SKETCH OF ENEMY'S WORKS AT BROOKLYN FERRY.
Crude, largely diagrammatic manuscript sketch of a fort. 7¼ x 8⅛. May 2, 1781. Library of Congress. Washington Papers (Vol. 172 p. 32148).

(5) (NEW YORK ISLAND AND BRITISH FORTIFICATIONS).
Crude manuscript sketch of Manhattan, lower Bronx and adjacent Long Island with location of defenses. 11½ x 15. November 28, 1782. Library of Congress. Washington Papers (60, 179).

(6) PLAN OF THE FORT ON LOYDS NECK—TAKEN BY A PERSON ON THE SPOT.
On verso. Rough manuscript sketch of the fort. 7¼ x 7¾. Library of Congress. Washington Papers (Vol. 145 p. 19326).

(7) A ROUGH DRAUGHT OF FORT ST. GEORGE ON THE SOUTH SIDE OF LONG ISLAND TAKEN BY SURPRISE BY A DETACHMENT OF TROOPS UNDER THE COMMAND OF MAJOR TALLMADGE ON THE 23RD OF NOVr 1780.
Rough, accurate manuscript sketch of the fort. 12¼ x 15½. Connecticut Historical Society (see also Washington Papers, Library of Congress 44, 52, 58).

(8) A ROUGH DRAUGHT OF FORT ST. GEORGE.
Rough manuscript sketch, less detailed than the similar sketch in the same hand in the Connecticut Historical Society. Enclosed in letter from Major Benjamin Tallmadge of Fairfield to General Washington at Preakness, November 25, 1780. Library of Congress, Washington Papers. (44, 52).

(9) DRAUGHT OF FORT SLONGO ON LONG ISLAND.
Rough manuscript sketch 7¾ x 9¾ with brief descriptive notes. By same hand on the two sketch maps of Fort St. George. Enclosed in letter from General Heath at Continental Village to General Washington near Yorktown, October 5, 1781. Library of Congress, Washington Papers. (52, 270).

(C) NEW JERSEY

(1) (TRENTON).
A rough but accurate pencil sketch of the village of Trenton 6½ x 7¾ showing main roads and buildings on verso of the "Order of March to Trenton Decr 25, 1776" of right-hand portion of sheet 4. Knox Papers, Massachusetts Historical Society. Note: I am indebted to Mr. Zach Taylor of Fair Haven, N. J. for this discovery.

(2) FROM SPRINGFIELD TO MORRISTOWN.
A careful manuscript road survey 8 x 8½. Sparks Manuscripts, Harvard University Library. PF 158.

(3) SKETCH OF ROADS ABOUT SPRINGFIELD, SCOTCH PLAINS &C.
A careful manuscript road survey 8 x 12½ by the same hand as the previous. Sparks Manuscripts, Harvard University Library.

(4) BATTLE OF MONMOUTH.
Rough sketch map 7¾ x 11, showing local knowledge and accurately placing the American but not the British forces. Historical Society of Pennsylvania. Photostat.

(D) PHILADELPHIA AND ENVIRONS

(1) PLAN OF THE REDOUBTS NEAR PHILADELPHIA 1ST APRIL 1778.
Careful manuscript survey 9½ x 15 of the British lines. On verso. "State of the British Lines and Country on the North April 1st 1778". Sparks Manuscripts, Harvard University Library. PF 158.

(2) MAP OF THE ENCAMPMENT AT VALLEY FORGE.
Careful, well finished ms. 14½ x 20½ with color wash. Carefully labeled. Historical Society of Pennsylvania. Am 602, 7.

(3) PLAN OF THE ATTACK ON MUD ISLAND IN THE DELAWARE NOVr 1777.
Careful manuscript map 8 x 13 with narrow border, great detail and careful labeling. "Esquisse des forts sur le delaware, Forts Mercer & Mifflin". On verso "esquisse du fort Mercer a Hogue le octobre 1777". "Plan of the redoubts on the Delaware called Fort Mercer which was captured by some Hessians under Count Donop October 1777". Historical Society of Pennsylvania. AM 602, 28.

(4) ENCAMPMENT AT VALLEY FORGE 1778.
Crude, poorly labeled ms. 12¾ x 15½ in borders. Historical Society of Pennsylvania. Am 602, 7.

(5) ROADS ABOUT SKIPPACK, GERMANTOWN &C TAKEN OCTOBER 1777.
Crude ms. 11¾ x 15½ showing troop concentration, positions of camps and movements from October 6 to November 15. Historical Society of Pennsylvania. Am 602, 31.

(6) ROADS ROUND PHILADELPHIA.
Crude ms. 12¾ x 16¼. Historical Society of Pennsylvania. Am 602, 25.

(7) PLAN OF GERMANTOWN BATTLE OF OCTOB. 1775.
On verso. Crude ms. accurately depicting the disposition of only the American forces. Irregular. 7 x 13½ overall. Huntington Library. HM 1515.

(E) SOUTHERN STATES

(1) PLAN OF GYWN'S ISLAND VIRGINIA JUNE 1776 OCCUPIED BY LORD DINSMORE & HIS CREW.
Careful, accurate ms. 12½ x 16½ without much detail. Sparks Manuscripts, Harvard University Library. PF 158.

(2) (NORFOLK, PORTSMOUTH AND THE ELISABETH RIVER).
Crude sketch map 8¼ x 12 showing disposition of troops, possibly by Benjamin Tallmadge. Library of Congress.

(3) PLAN OF THE ROUTE OF THE ENEMY FROM CHARLOTTE 12TH OCTOBER 1780.
"Nelson fecit, non fecit scripsit". Rough manuscript 9 x 13¾. Sparks Collection, Cornell University Library. MPI 551.

(4) (MAP OF THE SIEGE OF YORKTOWN).
Very crude, highly diagrammatic sketch plan 8 x 9¾ showing disposition of troops. May have been made by John Cocke. Yale University Library. *783nc/Y82/1781D.

(5) (YORKTOWN AND GLOUCESTER).
Rough wood cut "Plan of the Investment of Yorktown and Glocester" on the title page of "The United States Almanack 1783" published by Andrew Beers. On the verso of the title page is an "Explanation of the Plan". Sinclair Hamilton Collection, Princeton University Library.

(6) (CHARLESTON AND SURROUNDING AREA).
Careful tracing of printed map. 11¾ x 12. Enclosed in a letter from General Lincoln to General Washington, August 3, 1781. Both were at or near Dobbs Ferry. Library of Congress. Washington Manuscripts. (181, 45).

To increase the utility of this volume which is essentially an index in itself, section references have been substituted for page references. A number has been assigned to the Introduction, to each map maker, and to the anonymous maps, the latter being additionally accorded regional subdivision by letter. For ease of use, the Table of Contents has been repeated below.

When referring to data contained in an individual's biography, "Bi" is used. If the reference is to a map, the map number is used. If there is only one map given for a particular map maker, it is presumed to be numbered (1). For example, under PISCATAWAY, N. J. is listed 3/Bi, indicating that a reference to this town is made in Antill's (3) biography (Bi).

— A —

ACADEMIE ROYAL DE PEINTURE ET DE SCULPTURE, PARIS, 26/Bi.
ACQUACKNUCK (ACQUACKONONCK, AQUACKNONK), 17/109, 27/79, 27/79B.
ADJUTSA, N. Y., 27/103D.
AIJ, FRANCE, 40/Bi.
AITKEN, ROBERT, 2/Bi, 16/Bi.
ALBANY, N. Y., 17/Bi, 17/93, 17/93A, 17/93B, 17/93C, 17/93D, 17/93E, 17/93F 17/93H, 17/93I, 17/93K, 17/93L, 17/93M, 17/93N, 17/93O, 17/93P, 17/93Q, 17/93R, 17/93S, 17/93T, 17/93U, 17/94, 21/52, 21/52A, 21/52B, 21/52C, 34/1, 37/2.
ALBANY COUNTY, N. Y., 17/Bi, 48/Bi, 48/1.
ALBI, FRANCE, 47/Bi.
ALEXANDER, JAMES, 17/Bi.
ALEXANDER, WILLIAM (LORD STIRLING), 17/Bi, 17/1st map, 34/1, 41/Bi.
ALEXANDRIA, VA., 14/124L, 14/124M, 31/Bi.
ALLEN'S ORDINARY, 14/124T, 14/124U.
ALLENTOWN, N. J., 17/87, 17/87G, 43/5B.
AMERICAN ANTIQUARIAN SOCIETY, 1, 42/1.
"(THE) AMERICAN MAGAZINE OR GENERAL REPOSITORY", 31/Bi.
"(THE) AMERICAN MILITARY POCKET ATLAS", 41/4.
AMERICAN PHILOSOPHICAL SOCIETY LIBRARY, see American Philosophical Society of Philadelphia.
AMERICAN PHILOSOPHICAL SOCIETY OF PHILADELPHIA, 1, 3/Bi, 5/Bi, 5/1, 8/Bi, 10/Bi, 14/Bi, 16/Bi, 17/Bi, 26/Bi, 31/Bi, 39/Bi, 41/Bi, 43/Bi, 46/Bi, 46/3, 49/Bi, 51/B12.

AMOS PETITS, 4/1C.
"AMPHITRITE", 18/Bi.
AMSTERDAM, 41/6, 41/7.
ANCHOR TAVERN, 14/124A, 14/124B.
ANDRE, MAJOR JOHN, 17/Bi, 42/Bi, 46/Bi.
ANDREW'S FORD, 14/130.
"ANNALS OF TRYON COUNTY", 18/2.
ANNAPOLIS, MD., 11/16.
ANTHONY'S NOSE, 17/84A.
ANTILL, EDWARD, 3/Bi.
APPLETON, N. Y. (OR CONDY, N. Y.), 17/96D.
ARCHIES, 17/86A.
ARMSTRONG, JOHN, 4/Bi, 17/Bi.
ARNOLD, BENEDICT, 1, 2/8, 3/Bi, 3/1, 5/Bi, 41/Bi.
ARTHUR KILL, 25/1.
AYLETT'S MILLS, 14/125B, 14/125C.
AYLETT'S WAREHOUSE, 14/125C.

— B —

BALTIMORE, MD., 14/124G, 14/124H.
BANCKER, ABRAHAM ("AMICUS REPUBLICAE"), 51/BB.
BARNEGAT INLET, N. J., 27/103A 2nd part.
BARRENHILL, PA. 11/3, 11/4, 11/5, 11/6, 11/7.
BASKING RIDGE, N. J., 12/1, 17/Bi, 17/70C.
BATTENKILL, N. Y., 48/Bi.
"BATTLE OF BUNKER'S HILL" (TRUMBULL), 46/Bi.
BAUMAN, SEBASTIAN, 5/Bi.
BAWBEE, HENRY, 6/Bi, 6/1.
BEACON HILL, BOSTON, MASS., 51/A3.
BEAMAN'S, N. J., 17/90C.
BEDFORD, N. Y., 17/24, 17/28, 17/32, 17/101, 17/102, 43/1.
BEDINI, SILVIO A., 1
BEERS, ANDREW, 51/E5.
BEERS, ELIAS, 41/5.
BEERS, ISAAC, 41/Bi.
BELLEGROVE, N. J. (BELLE GROVE, N. J.), 17/108, 50/3.
BEMIS HEIGHTS, MASS., 26/Bi, 37/2.
BERGEN COUNTY, N. J., 50/3.
BERGENFIELD, N. J. (SCHRALENBURG, N. J.), 32/Bi.
BERKELEY, BISHOP GEORGE, 11/13.
BETHLEHEM, PA. 17/57, 17/58, 17/69, 17/69-10th, 43/5B.
BEVERLY ROBINSON'S, 41/5.
BEVERLY'S MILL, 14/125D.
BIBOUTS, JOHN, 17/70C.
"BICKERSTAFF'S NEW-ENGLAND ALMANACK FOR THE YEAR OF OUR LORD, 1776", 51/A3.
BILLINGSPORT, N. J., 24/Bi.
BLACK HORSE, N. J., 17/87G.
BLACK RIVER, N. J., 14/117, 14/117C.
BLADENSBURGH, MD., 14/124K, 14/124L, 14/125H, 14/125I.
BLOOMERS MILL, 17/20.
BOHEMIA, MD., 9/1.
BONAPARTE, NAPOLEON, 7/Bi.
BONUMTOWN, N. J. (BONHAMTOWN, N. J.), 17/74E.
BOONTON, N. J., 17/90B.
BOSTON, MASS., 1, 2/2, 2/8, 7/Bi, 7/1, 25/Bi, 33/Bi, 33/1, 37/Bi, 41/Bi, 41/3, 42/Bi, 46/Bi, 46/1, 49/1, 51/A2, 51/A3.
BOSTON ATHENAEUM, 1.
"(THE) BOSTON DIRECTORY", 33/Bi.
"BOSTON GAZETTE AND COUNTRY JOURNAL", 41/5.
BOSTON GRENADIER CORPS, 25/Bi.
BOSTON HARBOR, MASS., 11/1, 28/Bi, 28/1, 51/A4.
"BOSTON MAGAZINE", 33/Bi.
BOSTON NECK, MASS., 2/3, 41/3, 46/Bi, 46/3.
BOSTON PUBLIC LIBRARY, 1, 25/1.
BOWDOIN COLLEGE, 7/Bi.
BOWDOIN, JAMES, 7/Bi, 7/1.
BOWDOIN, GOVERNOR JAMES, 7/Bi.
BOWEN, G. H., 18/1.
BOTTLE HILL, N. J., 17/75, 17/75A, 17/104C.
BOUND BROOK, N. J. (BOUNDBROOK, N. J.), 17/70F, 17/71B, 17/74.
BOURBON ISLAND, 18/Bi.
BOWLING GREEN ORDINARY, 14/124O, 14/124P.

"DEATH OF MONTGOMERY" (TRUMBULL), 46/Bi.
DE BRAHM, FERDINAND, 8/Bi, 41/Bi, 41/4.
DeGRASSE, COUNT, 1.
DELAWARE, 14/124B, 39/Bi, 41/7.
DELAWARE BAY, 2/8.
DELAWARE RIVER, 1, 14/115, 17/65, 18/3, 21/52C-2nd piece,
    27/103A, 31/1, 47/Bi, 47/1, 51/D3.
DENISON, J. (JOSEPH DENISON II, JOSEPH DENISON), 13/Bi.
DENNISON, ZINA, 41/5.
DERBY, PA., 14/124A.
D'ESTAING, COUNT, 1.
DETROIT, MICH., 6/1.
DeWITT, DR. ANDREW, 14/Bi.
DeWITT, RICHARD VARICK, 14/Bi.
DeWITT, SIMEON, 4/1, 14/Bi, 17/Bi, 17/46-2nd, 17/66, 17/106,
    21/52, 27/Bi, 30/Bi, 32/Bi, 36/1, 38/1, 43/3, 43/4, 43/5, 48/1,
    50/1, 50/2.
DIKINS MILLS, N. J., 17/71C.
DINSMORE, LORD, 51/E1.
DOBBS FERRY, N. Y., 15/Bi, 17/9, 17/15, 17/16, 17/110, 17/112B,
    17/113, 17/114, 22/1, 51/E6.
DONOP, COUNT VON, 51/D3.
DORCHESTER HEIGHTS, MASS., 25/Bi.
DOVER, N. Y., 43/1.
DOYLE'S INDEPENDENT RIFLE COMPANY, 30/Bi.
DOYLES TAVERN, 17/73-1st, 17/73-2nd.
DUANSBURG, N. Y., 21/52B.
DUBLIN, IRELAND, 31/Bi.
DUMFRIES, VA., 14/124N
DUNCASTLE (ALIAS BIRD'S ORDINARY), 14/124T, 14/125A.
DUNDERBERG, N. Y. (BEAR MOUNTAIN, N. Y.), 17/C, 41/2.
DUNFERMLINE, SCOTLAND, 17/Bi.
DUNMORE, LORD, 16/1.
DUPORTAIL, LOUIS, 15/Bi, 20/Bi, 47/2, 47/3.
DURHAM, N. H., 42/Bi.
DuSIMITIERE, PIERRE-EUGENE, 16/Bi.
DUYCKINKS MILL, PA., 17/70, 17/71, 17/72.

— E —

EAST CHESTER, N. Y., 17/10, 17/19.
EAST GREENWICH, R. I., 45/Bi.
EASTON, PA., 17/B, 17/68, 17/69-9th, 17/77, 17/77C, 17/83,
    17/91A, 17/92D, 17/92E, 17/92F, 17/92G, 43/5A, 51/B2.
EGMONT, LORD, 41/Bi.
ELIZABETH, N. J. (ELIZABETHTOWN, N. J.), 17/74, 17/74C, 17/75B,
    17/100-1st.
ELIZABETH RIVER, 51/E2.
ELIZABETH TOWN POINT, N. J., 17/82, 27/79, 27/79A.
ELK, HEAD OF, 14/124C, 14/124D.
ELKRIDGE, MD., 14/124H, 14/125K.
ELK RIVER, 9/1.
ENGLAND, 29/Bi, 33/Bi, 41/Bi, 43/Bi.
ERSKINE, ROBERT, 4/Bi, 4/1, 14/Bi, 14/66, 17/Bi, 17/1st map,
    17/A, 17/2nd unnumbered map; 17/3rd unnumbered map, 17/54,
    17/102, 17/105, 17/111, 17/112, 17/112B, 17/114, 20/Bi, 21/52,
    27/Bi, 27/79A, 30/Bi, 36/Bi, 36/1, 38/Bi, 38/1, 39/Bi, 39/1st
    map, 39/89A, 43/Bi, 43/1, 43/2, 43/3, 43/4, 43/5, 48/Bi, 48/1,
    50/Bi, 50/1, 50/2, 50/4.
ESTHER TOWN, N. Y., 27/103B.
EVANS, CHARLES, "AMERICAN BIBLIOGRAPHY", 41/5.
EVANS, LEWIS, 2/8, 17/Bi.

— F —

FAIRFIELD, CONN., 51/BB8.
FALMOUTH, VA., 14/124O.
FARMINGTON, CONN., 36/1.
FARMINGTON RIVER, 17/Bi, 36/1.
FISHER, JOSHUA, 2/8.
FISHKILL, N. Y., 17/29, 17/35, 17/38, 17/93, 17/93L, 17/93N,
    17/93O, 17/93P, 17/93Q, 17/93R, 17/93S, 17/93T, 17/93U,
    17/93V, 17/94, 43/5D.
FISHKILL RIVER, 14/131, 17/Bi, 17/C.
FLANDERS, N. J., 14/117A, 14/117B.

FLEURY, FRANCOIS LOUIS TEISSEIDRE DE (DE FLEURY, ALSO HENRY),
    18/Bi, 18/1, 18/2, 18/4.
FLORIDA, 14/128, 14/128-2nd, 14/128-3rd, 41/Bi, 41/4.
FORCE'S "AMERICAN ARCHIVES", 34/1, 41/2.
FT. ARNOLD, 11/14, 17/C, 47/4, 51/B4.
FT. CLINTON, see FT. Arnold.
FT. CONSTITUTION, 32/Bi, 32/1, 34/1, 41/Bi, 41/1, 41/2, 41/5,
    47/4, 51/B4, 51/B5, 51/B6, 51/B7.
FT. GEORGE, 41/Bi.
FT. LEE, 17/36, 50/1, 50/3.
FT. MERCER, 51/C3.
FT. MIFFLIN, 15/Bi, 18/Bi, 18/4, 18/5, 18/6, 51/C3.
FT. MONTGOMERY, 17/C, 17/1, 17/1B part 2, 17/2, 17/3, 29/Bi,
    34/Bi, 34/1, 44/Bi, 44/1.
FT. NEWPORT, 18/2.
FT. PITT, 1, 6/1.
FT. PUTNAM, 26/4, 47/4.
FT. REED, 17/96B 2nd.
FT. ST. GEORGE, 51/BB7, 51/BB8, 51/BB9.
FT. SCHUYLER, 18/1, 18/2.
FT. SLONGO, 51/BB9.
FT. SULLIVAN, 17/96, 17/96A, 23/10.
FT. TICONDEROGA, 41/Bi.
FT. WASHINGTON, 8/1, 32/Bi, 51/B14.
FRANCE, 1, 11/Bi, 11/19, 15/Bi, 18/Bi, 24/Bi, 31/Bi, 43/Bi.
FRANKFURT-AM-MAIN, GERMANY, 5/Bi.
FRANKLIN, BENJAMIN, 9/Bi, 17/Bi, 24/1, 39/Bi.
FRANKLIN, GOVERNOR WILLIAM, 17/Bi.
FRASER, ALEXANDER, 19/Bi, 19/1.
FREDERICKSBURG, N. Y., 17/29, 17/30.
FREDERICKSBURGH, VA., 14/124O.
FREEMAN'S FARM, 37/2.
FRENCH ASSEMBLY, 20/Bi.
FRENCH AND INDIAN WAR, 1, 2/8, 5/Bi, 17/Bi, 37/Bi.
FRENCH HYDROGRAPHIC SERVICE, 11/14.
FRENCH INDIA, 18/Bi.
FRENCH MINISTRY OF WAR AND FRENCH WAR OFFICE, 11/9, 11/16.
FRENCH REPUBLICAN ARMY, 24/Bi.

— G —

GAGE, GENERAL THOMAS, 2/3.
GAGLISUQUILAKENY, N. Y., 23/26.
GAINE, HUGH, 51/A2.
GANSEVOORT, COLONEL PETER, 18/1, 18/2.
GARDINER'S ORDINARY, 14/125D.
GARRISON'S TAVERN, 17/71B, 17/80.
GATES, GENERAL HORATIO, 17/14, 26/Bi, 37/Bi, 41/Bi, 46/Bi.
GENESSEE, N. Y., 17/96B 2nd, 17/97, 17/97A, 17/97B, 23/27.
GENESSEE COUNTRY, 29/Bi.
GENEVA, SWITZERLAND, 16/Bi.
"GENTLEMAN'S MAGAZINE", 2/2.
GEORGETOWN, MD., 14/124L.
GEORGIA, 2/1, 41/Bi, 41/4.
"GEOGRAPHICAL GAZETTEER OF MASSACHUSETTS", 33/Bi.
GERMAN FUSILIERS, 5/Bi.
GERMANTOWN, PA., 10/Bi, 17/70, 17/70A, 17/72, 17/72B, 23/Bi.
    39/Bi, 51/C5, 51/C7.
GIBBS' "DOCUMENTARY HISTORY", 8/Bi.
GILL'S FORD, 14/130.
GLISVELLE, FRANCE, 20/Bi.
GLOUCESTER, N. J., 17/Bi.
GLOUCESTER, VA., 5/2, 5/3, 5/4, 11/2, 51/E5.
GORDON, THOMAS, 43/1, 43/2.
GOSHEN, N. Y., 14/128, 14/128-2nd, 14/128-3rd, 14/128-4th.
GOTHAM, N. J., 27/79B, 27/79C.
GOUVION, JEAN-BAPTISTE DE, 15/Bi, 20/Bi.
GOVERNOR'S BRIDGE, 14/124K.
GRANT, GENERAL JAMES, 11/3, 11/4, 11/5, 11/6, 11/7.
GRAY, CAPTAIN WILLIAM, 14/130, 17/Bi, 17/C, 17/52, 21/Bi,
    21/52.
GREAT FALLS, N. J., 17/47-2nd, 17/56, 17/56B.
GREEN, T., 41/5.
GREENE, GENERAL NATHANIEL, 1, 12/Bi, 12/1, 26/Bi, 40/1.

LIBRARY COMPANY OF PHILADELPHIA, 1, 16/Bi.
LIBRARY OF CONGRESS, 1, 6/1, 7/1, 10/1, 11/14, 14/Bi, 15/2, 15/3, 16/Bi, 17/112B, 37/2, 40/1, 41/6, 41/8, 46/1, 47/2, 47/3, 49/1, 49/2, 50/3, 50/4, 51/A2, 51/B2, 51/BB1, 51/BB2, 51/BB3, 51/BB4, 51/BB5, 51/BB6, 51/BB7, 51/BB8, 51/BB9, 51/E2, 51/E6.
LIBRARY OF FORT MONROE, VA., 5/3.
"LIFE OF JOSEPH BRANT", 18/2.
LINCOLN, GENERAL BENJAMIN, 51/B1, 51/E6.
LITCHFIELD, CONN., 17/54.
LITTLE BRITAIN MEETING HOUSE, 14/130-2nd.
LITTLE FALLS, N. J., 17/67A, 17/109.
LIVINGSTON, 34/Bi.
LODGE, BENJAMIN, 17/Bi, 17/C, 17/79, 17/90B, 17/103, 27/Bi.
LONDON, ENGLAND, 17/Bi, 46/Bi.
LONG ISLAND, N. Y., 8/1, 11/19, 14/66, 17/Bi, 17/B part 1, 20/Bi, 25/Bi, 35/1, 42/Bi, 42/1, 51/B12, 51/BB, 51/BB5, 51/BB7, 51/BB9.
LONG POND, N. J., 17/Bi, 17/53.
LONGWOOD, N. J., 17/90C.
LOTTS, 17/47.
LOUISBOURG, NOVA SCOTIA, 2/8.
LOUISIANA, 1.
LOUNSBURY, MICHAEL, 17/23.
LOVELL, GENERAL SOLOMON (LOVEL), 51/A1.
LOWER FORGE, 17/53.
LOWNES, CALEB, 28/Bi.
LLOYD'S NECK, N. Y. (LOYD'S NECK, N. Y.), 51/BB6.

— M —

McDOUGALL, GENERAL ALEXANDER, 26/2.
McMURRAY, WILLIAM, 17/70C, 30/Bi, 30/1.
MACE'S TAVERN, 17/51.
MACHIN, THOMAS, 29/Bi. 29/1, 44/Bi.
MACHIN, GENERAL THOMAS, 29/Bi, 41/Bi.
MAGABADUCE, MAINE, 51/A1.
MAINE, 25/Bi, 42/Bi.
MALCOLM'S CONTINENTAL REGIMENT, 50/Bi.
MAMARONECK, N. Y., 17/8.
MANHATTAN, see New York City.
MARIETTA, OHIO, 37/Bi.
MARTELEER'S ROCK, N. Y., 41/2.
MARYLAND, 1, 14/127, 17/Bi, 41/7.
MASSACHUSETTS HISTORICAL SOCIETY, 1, 13/1, 26/4, 44/1, 51/A4, 51/C1.
MATTAPONI RIVER (MATTEPOYNE, MATTEPONYE), 14/124O, 14/124P.
MAUMEE INDIANS, 37/Bi.
MAURITIUS ISLAND, 18/Bi.
MELLON COLLECTION, 41/5.
MERCEREAU, JOHN, 51/BB.
MERCEREAU, JOSHUA, 51/BB.
MEREDECUN, VA., 14/124R.
MEZIERES, FRANCE, 11/Bi, 15/Bi, 20/Bi.
MIDDLEBROOK, N. J., 17/76.
MIDDLE BUSH, N. J., 14/121.
MIFFLIN, THOMAS, 46/3.
MILES PENNSYLVANIA RIFLE REGIMENT, 12/Bi, 21/Bi.
MILFORD, MASS. (MENDON, MASS.), 42/Bi.
MILLIDGE, THOMAS, 1.
MILLSTONE COURTHOUSE, N. J., 12/1.
MIRES, JACOB, 17/57C.
MOHAWK RIVER, 18/2, 21/52C, 48/Bi.
MOHOPACK POND, N. Y., 14/131.
MONMOUTH, BATTLE OF, 11/8, 11/9, 11/10, 18/Bi, 25/Bi, 51/C4.
MONMOUTH COUNTY, N. J., 1.
MONS, BATTLE OF, 18/Bi.
MONTEGO BAY, JAMAICA, 41/Bi.
MONTGOMERY, GENERAL RICHARD, 3/Bi, 44/1.
MONTMEDY BATTLE, 18/Bi.
MONTREAL, CANADA, 2/6, 3/Bi.
MOORE'S LAND, 14/129.
MOORESTOWN, N. J. (MOORSTOWN, N. J.), 17/87F.

MORGAN'S RIFLES, 24/Bi.
MOROSCOSICK, VA., 14/125C.
MORRELL'S TAVERN, 17/71C.
MORRISTOWN, N. J., 4/Bi, 4/1, 4/1A, 4/1C, 7/1, 12/1, 14/106A, 14/106B, 17/46-1st, 17/47, 17/70B, 17/70C, 17/73-1st, 17/73-2nd, 17/73-3rd, 17/73-4th, 17/73-5th, 17/73-6th, 17/73-7th, 17/75, 17/75A, 17/76, 17/77, 17/77D, 17/90A, 17/90B, 17/90C, 17/104, 17/104B, 17/104D, 17/105, 17/111, 25/1, 40/1, 51/C2.
MORRISTOWN NATIONAL HISTORICAL PARK LIBRARY, 1.
MORSE'S "THE AMERICAN UNIVERSAL GEOGRAPHY", 13/Bi.
MOTHERELLS TAVERN, 14/130.
MOUNTAIN MEETING PLACE, 17/104C.
MOUNT BETHEL MEETING HOUSE, N. J., 17/70D.
MOUNT DEFIANCE, N. Y., 46/5.
MOUNT HOLLY, N. J., 17/87, 43/5C.
MT. PLEASANT, N. J., 14/117, 17/90C.
MOUZON (SURVEYOR), 41/4.
MUD ISLAND, PA., 18/Bi, 18/3, 47/1, 47/2, 51/D3.
MURDERS KILL, N. Y. (MURDERERS KILL, MURDERS CREEK, N. Y.), 17/C, 41/5.
MURRAY'S "AN IMPARTIAL HISTORY OF THE PRESENT WAR IN AMERICA", 33/Bi.
MUSCANECUNK MOUNTAIN, PA., 17/77, 17/77C.
MUSCONETEUNK, N. J., 4/1B.

— N —

NANTICOKE CREEK, PA., 27/103A-2nd route.
NANTICOKE FALLS, PA., 17/95I.
NARRAGANSETT BAY, R. I., 13/1, 13/2, 37/Bi, 37/1.
NASHUAN ISLAND, MASS., 7/Bi.
NATIONAL ARCHIVES, 1, 20/1.
NAVESINK HIGHLANDS, N. J., 17/54.
NELSON (MAPMAKER), 51/E3.
NESHANIC RIVER, N. J. (NEWSHANNOCK, N. J.), 17/73-4th.
NETHERLANDS, 41/Bi.
NEVIL, JAMES, 43/Bi.
NEWARK, N. J., 17/67B, 17/104C, 25/1, 27/79, 27/79A, 27/79B.
NEWBERRY LIBRARY, 1, 51/B1.
NEW BRUNSWICK, N. J., 12/1, 17/70D, 17/70E, 17/74D, 17/74E, 17/74F, 17/87, 17/111, 43/4B, 43/5B.
NEWBURGH, N. Y. (NEW BOROUGH, NEWBOROUGH, N. Y.), 17/C, 17/2nd unnumbered map, 17/3rd unnumbered map, 17/5, 17/6, 17/7, 17/36, 17/37, 17/93, 17/93A, 17/93B, 17/93C, 17/93D, 17/93V, 17/94, 29/Bi, 29/1, 43/2.
NEWCASTLE, DEL., 9/1.
NEW CASTLE, VA., 14/124R.
NEW ENGLAND, 2/8, 40/Bi, 51/A.
NEW FAIRFIELD, CONN., 17/2nd unnumbered map.
NEWFOUNDLAND, CANADA, 2/8.
NEWFOUNDLAND, N. J., 17/111.
NEW GERMANTOWN, N. J., 14/117, 14/119, 14/119F.
NEW HAVEN, CONN., 17/101, 17/102, 41/5, 41/6, 41/7.
NEW JERSEY (THE JERSEYS), 4/Bi, 11/2, 11/19, 14/66, 14/106A, 14/106B, 17/Bi, 17/1st map, 17/A, 17/B part 1, 17/3rd unnumbered map, 17/81, 17/100-1st, 27/103A 2nd part, 30/1, 38/Bi, 41/7, 42/Bi, 42/1, 43/1, 43/4, 43/4A, 43/4B, 43/4C, 51/B12, 51/B14.
NEW JERSEY BILL IN CHANCERY, 2/8.
NEW JERSEY HISTORICAL SOCIETY, 1, 17/Bi.
"NEW-JERSEY JOURNAL", 5/Bi.
NEW JERSEY STATE LIBRARY, 1.
NEW KENT COURT HOUSE, 14/124S.
"NEW LONDON GAZETTE", 41/6.
NEW LONDON HARBOR, CONN., 46/4.
NEW MILFORD, CONN., 17/39.
NEWPORT, DEL., 14/124B.
NEWPORT, R. I., 11/13.
NEWPORT PRESERVATION SOCIETY, see Preservation Society of Newport County, Newport, R. I.
NEWTON, N. J. (NEWTOWN, N. J), 17/43A, 17/43B.
NEWTON, N. Y., 17/96, 17/96B, 17/96I, 17/96K, 23/15.
NEWTOWN, MD., 14/124F.

NEW WINDSOR, N. Y., 6/1, 14/128, 14/128-2nd, 14/128-3rd, 17/Bi, 17/A, 17/C, 17/D, 17/E, 17/41, 17/51, 30/1, 32/Bi, 41/1, 41/2.
NEW YORK BAY, 1, 17/B part 1.
NEW YORK BUREAU OF SURPLUS REAL PROPERTY, 1.
NEW YORK CAMPAIGN, 8/1, 8/2, 51/B12.
NEW YORK CITY, N. Y. (MANHATTAN, N. Y.), 5/Bi, 11/19, 14/66, 16/Bi, 17/Bi, 17/1st map, 17/A, 17/2nd unnumbered map, 17/37, 18/2, 27/103A 2nd part, 37/Bi, 40/Bi, 40/2, 41/Bi, 41/3, 42/Bi, 42/1, 46/Bi, 46/6, 50/Bi, 51/B11, 51/B12, 51/B14, 51/BB, 51/BB1, 51/BB2, 51/BB3, 51/BB5.
"NEW YORK GAZETTE", 41/3.
NEW YORK HISTORICAL SOCIETY, 1, 4/1C, 14/Bi, 17/Bi, 19/1, 21/Bi, 26/2, 26/3, 26/4, 30/1, 36/1, 38/1, 43/1, 43/2, 43/3, 43/4, 50/1, 50/2.
NEW YORK MARINE SOCIETY, 41/Bi.
NEW YORK PUBLIC LIBRARY, 1, 8/3, 17/2nd unnumbered map, 18/2, 15/B13.
NEW YORK STATE, 3/Bi, 5/Bi, 11/19, 14/Bi, 17/Bi, 17/1st map, 17/3rd unnumbered map, 17/100-1st, 29/1, 43/1, 43/2, 51/B.
NEW YORK STATE LIBRARY, 29/Bi, 34/Bi.
NEW YORK SECRETARY OF STATE, 34/1.
NEW YORK THRUWAY, 30/1.
NIAGARA RIVER (NIAGRA RIVER), 17/63.
NICHOL'S HILL, 17/1D.
NICOLA, LEWIS, 31/Bi.
NICOLL, ISAAC, 32/Bi, 32/1, 34/Bi.
NOEL (PRINTER), 41/3.
NORFOLK, VA., 51/E2.
NORMAN, JOHN, 33/Bi.
NORRISTOWN, PA., 39/89B.
"NORTH AMERICAN'S ALMANACK", ISAAC WARREN, 51/B11.
NORTH CAROLINA, 1, 2/1, 41/4.
NORTHUMBERLAND, N. J., 17/91B.
NORWALK, CONN., 17/101, 17/102.
NORWICH, CONN., 41/5.
NOTTINGHAM IRON WORKS, 14/124F, 14/124G.
NOVA SCOTIA, 2/8.

— O —

OGDENS COALHOUSE, 17/46-2nd.
OGLETHORPE, JAMES, 41/Bi.
OHIO COMPANY OF VOLUNTEERS, 37/Bi.
OLNEY, CAPTAIN STEPHEN, 45/Bi.
ONANAUGHQUAGO, N. Y. (ONONOUGHQUA, N. Y.), 17/65, 21/52C 2nd piece.
ONEIDA COUNTY, N. Y., 29/Bi.
ONTARIO LAKE, 18/2, 27/103A 2nd part.
ORANGE COUNTY, N. Y., 38/Bi, 50/3.
ORANGE LAKE, N. Y., 29/Bi.
ORLÉANS, FRANCE, 15/Bi.
OXFORD UNIVERSITY, 7/Bi.

— P —

PAINE, THOMAS, 2/Bi.
PALISADES, N. J., 14/128-5th.
PALMER, THOMAS, 34/Bi, 34/1, 41/2.
PAMUNKY RIVER, 14/124Q, 14/125A.
PARAMUS, N. J., 14/116, 17/56, 17/56A, 17/56B, 17/110, 17/113, 17/114.
PARIS, FRANCE, 11/10.
PASSAIC, N. J. (PASSAICK, N. J.), 14/106A, 14/106B, 14/116, 17/47-2nd, 17/67, 17/67A.
PAULUS HOOK, N. J., 15/3, 17/2nd unnumbered map.
PEACH BOTTOM FERRY, 14/130-2nd.
PEALE, CHARLES WILSON, 51/B12.
PEEKSKILL, N. Y., 14/131, 17/C, 17/1, 17/6, 17/7, 17/8, 17/30, 17/45, 17/50A, 17/50B.
PENNSYLVANIA, 1, 4/Bi, 14/66, 14/127, 17/Bi, 18/5, 28/Bi, 39/Bi, 41/7, 42/Bi, 43/Bi, 47/2, 49/2.
PENNSYLVANIA HISTORICAL SOCIETY, see Historical Society of Pennsylvania.
"PENNSYLVANIA MAGAZINE OR AMERICAN MONTHLY MUSEUM", 2/Bi, 2/1, 2/2, 2/3, 2/4, 2/5, 2/6, 2/7, 2/8, 16/1, 28/1.

"PENNSYLVANIA MAGAZINE OF HISTORY AND BIOGRAPHY", 23/Bi.
PENNYTOWN, N. J. (PENNINGTON, N. J.), 17/87, 17/87A, 17/87E.
PENOBSCOT INDIANS, 25/Bi.
PENOBSCOT RIVER, 51/A1.
PENSACOLA, FLORIDA, 1, 41/Bi.
PERRIER (ENGRAVER), 11/5.
PERTH AMBOY, N. J., 12/1, 14/106A, 14/106B, 17/74D, 17/100-1st, 17/111, 24/Bi, 24/1, 43/3, 43/4A.
PETER SCHUYLERS, 17/48-2nd.
PHILADELPHIA, PA., 1, 2/Bi, 2/8, 5/Bi, 5/2, 9/Bi, 9/1, 10/Bi, 14/Bi, 14/66, 14/124A, 15/Bi, 16/Bi, 17/Bi, 17/57A, 17/57B, 17/87, 17/87E, 18/Bi, 18/7, 23/Bi, 24/Bi, 27/103A 2nd part, 28/Bi, 31/Bi, 31/1, 33/Bi, 39/Bi, 41/7, 41/8, 43/Bi, 43/5C, 47/1, 51/B1, 51/D1, 51/D6.
PHILADELPHIA COMMITTEE OF SAFETY, 10/Bi.
PHILIPSE, N. Y., 51/B13.
PHILLIPS, JOSEPH, 35/Bi, 35/1.
PICKERING, TIMOTHY, 42/Bi.
PIERPONT MORGAN LIBRARY, 1, 17/Bi, 17/1st map.
PISCATAWAY, N. J., 3/Bi, 14/125G, 14/125H, 17/74E.
PITHIVIENS, FRANCE, 15/Bi.
PITTSTOWN, N. J., 14/119, 14/119C.
PLUCKEMIN, N. J., 14/117, 14/117C, 17/70B, 17/76, 17/111, 43/4B.
PLYMOUTH, MASS., 42/Bi.
PLYMOUTH, N. H., 42/Bi.
POCONO MOUNTAINS, PA., 27/103A.
POIN'S "PRACTICAL BUILDER", 33/Bi.
POINT BATTERY, N. Y., 51/B14.
POLAND, 26/Bi.
POLOPAN ISLAND, N. Y., 51/B3.
POLYPHENES ISLAND, N. Y., 22/1.
POMPTON PLAINS, N. J., 17/42, 17/46-1st, 17/56, 17/56A, 17/56B, 17/67, 17/90A, 43/4A, 43/4C, 50/4.
POMPTON RIVER, 17/90A.
PONDICHERY REGIMENT, 18/Bi.
POND'S CHURCH, 17/56A.
PORT ROYAL, VA., 14/125D, 14/125E.
PORT TOBACCO, VA., 14/125F, 14/125G.
PORTER, ELIJAH, 17/Bi, 17/40, 36/Bi, 36/1.
PORTSMOUTH, VA., 51/E2.
POTTERSTOWN, PA., 17/72, 17/72B, 17/77, 17/77A, 17/77B.
POTOMAC RIVER, 14/125E.
POUGHKEEPSIE, N. Y., 17/93T, 32/Bi.
POWNALL, THOMAS, 17/Bi.
PREAKNESS, N. J., 51/BB8.
PRESERVATION SOCIETY OF NEWPORT COUNTY, NEWPORT, R. I., 1, 11/11.
PRINCETON, N. J., 10/Bi, 10/1, 14/121A, 14/121B, 17/80, 35/1.
PRINCETON UNIVERSITY LIBRARY, 1, 12/1, 51/A3, 51/B11, 51/E5.
PRINGLE, SIR JOHN, 17/Bi.
PROSPECT HILL, MASS., 46/1.
PROVINCE ISLANDS, PA., 47/2.
PULASKI, GENERAL CASIMIR, 18/Bi.
PUPLOPES POINT, N. Y., 34/1.
PURDY, ANDREW, 17/22.
PURISBURG, S. C., 8/3.
PUTNAM, RUFUS, 37/Bi, 37/1.
PYE, DAVID, 17/Bi, 17/27, 38/Bi, 38/1.

— Q —

QUAKER HILL, N. Y., 17/29, 17/49.
QUEBEC, CANADA, 2/7, 2/8, 3/Bi, 3/1, 41/Bi.
QUEEN'S COLLEGE (RUTGERS UNIVERSITY), 14/Bi.
QUIALUTEMUNK, N. J., 23/3.
QUIBBLETOWN, N. J. (NEWMARKET, N. J.), 17/67D, 17/70C, 17/70D, 17/74, 43/3.

— R —

RADIERE, see La Radiere.
RAHWAY, N. J., 17/75C.
RAMAPO VALLEY, N. J., 30/1.
RAM GARRISONS, 17/87A.
RANDOLPH, RICHARD, 5/1.

RAPPAHANNOCK RIVER, 14/125D.
RARITAN BAY, 11/19.
RARITAN RIVER, 12/1, 17/71, 17/71C, 17/73-4th, 17/73-6th, 25/1.
RAUSON'S ORDINARY, THOMAS, 14/124S, 14/124T.
READING, PA., 39/1st map, 43/Bi.
REDDINGTON, N. J., 17/77, 17/77B, 17/77E, 43/4A.
RED HOOK, N. Y., 17/93P, 17/93Q, 51/B14.
REED, JOHN F., 11/15.
RENOW DOCK, 17/C.
RHINEBECK, N. Y., (RHYNBECK, N. Y.), 17/93R.
RHINELANDER, FREDERICK, 34/Bi.
RHODE ISLAND, 11/11, 11/12, 11/13, 13/1, 13/2, 18/Bi, 46/Bi, 51/A6.
RHODE ISLAND SECRETARY OF STATE, 1, 13/2.
RIDGEFIELD, CONN., 17/28.
RINGOES, N. J., 14/119, 14/119C, 14/119D, 17/73-3rd, 17/73-4th.
RINGWOOD, N. J., 17/Bi, 17/41, 17/42, 17/53.
RISTOW, DR. WALTER W., 1, 14/Bi.
RITTENHOUSE, DAVID, 14/127, 17/Bi, 39/Bi, 39/1st map, 39/89A.
RIVINGTON, JAMES, 41/3.
ROBERTSONS AND TRUMBULL, 51/A3.
ROBINSONS MILLS, 17/38, 17/45.
ROBINSON'S STORES, 17/43E.
ROCHAMBEAU, GENERAL JEAN BAPTISTE DONATIEN, 1, 18/Bi, 20/1, 40/2.
ROCHEFONTAINE, ETIENNE NICOLAS MARIE BÉCHET DE, 40/Bi, 40/1, 40/2.
ROCKAWAY BRIDGE, N. J., 17/48-1st.
ROCKAWAY RIVER, 17/90B.
ROE, AUSTIN ("724"), 51/BB.
ROMANS, BERNARD, 41/Bi, 41/1, 41/2, 41/3, 41/4, 41/7, 44/Bi.
ROMANS, HUBERTUS, 41/Bi.
ROWLING'S TAVERN, 14/124H.
ROYAL AMERICAN GOVERNMENT, 31/Bi.
ROYAL SOCIETY, 17/Bi.
ROXBURY, MASS., 46/1.
RUFFIN'S FERRY, 14/125A.
RUSSIA, 24/Bi.
RYE NECK, N. Y., 17/20.

— S —

SADDLE RIVER, N. J., 50/4.
ST. AUGUSTINE, FLA., 41/4.
ST. CLAIR, GENERAL ARTHUR, 42/Bi, 51/B1.
ST. HIPPOLYTE, LANGUEDOC PROVINCE, FRANCE, 18/Bi.
ST. JOHNS, CANADA, 3/Bi.
ST. LAWRENCE RIVER, 2/8.
ST. PAUL'S CHURCH, N. Y., 40/Bi.
ST. PETER'S CHURCHYARD, PHILADELPHIA, PA., 16/Bi, 23/Bi.
SANDY HOOK, N. J., 17/Bi, 17/B part 1.
SANTO DOMINGO, 40/Bi.
SARATOGA CAMPAIGN, 14/Bi, 26/Bi, 26/1, 37/Bi, 42/Bi.
SAVANNAH, BATTLE OF, 19/Bi, 19/1.
SAW MILL RIVER, 14/120, 17/13, 17/16, 17/17, 17/59.
SAW-PITTS, 17/24.
SAYER, R. AND BENNETT, J., 41/4, 42/Bi.
SCAMMELL, ALEXANDER, 42/Bi, 42/1.
SCHOHARIE, N. Y. (SCOHARIE, N. Y.), 17/Bi, 21/52, 21/52A 21/52B, 21/52C.
SCHUYLER, GENERAL PHILIP, 3/Bi.
SCHUYLKILL RIVER, 17/Bi, 17/87E, 27/103A, 31/1, 39/1st map, 39/89A, 39/89B, 47/2.
SCOT, ROBERT, 5/Bi, 5/2.
SCOTCH PLAINS, N. J., 17/67, 17/67C, 17/67D, 17/107, 51/C3.
SCULL, NICHOLAS, 43/Bi.
SCULL, WILLIAM, 14/124C, 17/Bi, 17/55, 17/98, 17/99, 43/Bi, 43/1, 43/2, 43/3, 43/4.
SEQUESTRATION COMMITTEE, 32/Bi.
SELLERS, HOLLAND, 51/Bi.
SENECA LAKE, 17/96C, 17/96D, 17/96E, 17/96F, 17/97, 27/103C, 27/last map, 51/B2.
SHESHECUNUNK, PA., 23/7

SHICKOHONNA, PA., 17/95H.
SHORT HILLS, N. J., 17/74B, 17/75C, 17/78.
SHREWSBURY, MD., 10/Bi.
SINCLAIR HAMILTON COLLECTION, see Princeton University Library.
SING SING, N. Y., 17/22.
SIPPINGWILLS, JAMES, 17/87F, 17/87G.
SKEEPACK, N. J. (SKIPPACK, N. J.), 17/73, 17/73 1st part, 51/C5.
SLACK'S FERRY, 17/87B.
SLATTOWN, N. J., 17/87G.
SMITH'S CLOVE ("CLOVE" OR "SLOTE" WERE USED TO INDICATE A NARROW CLEFT, GAP OR NOTCH), 17/C, 17/4, 17/5, 17/41, 17/85, 30/1.
SMITH, WILLIAM, 44/Bi, 44/1.
SNEED'S ORDINARY, 14/125D.
SNOWDEN'S IRON WORKS, 14/125K.
SOLOTHURN, SWITZERLAND, 26/Bi.
SOMERSET, N. J., 17/74F, 17/80.
SOMERSET COURT HOUSE, N. J., 17/71B, 17/87.
SOMERVILLE, N. J., 14/106A, 14/106B.
"SORRELL", CANADA, 41/Bi.
SOUTHBURY, CONN., 17/43C, 17/43D.
SOUTH CAROLINA, 2/1, 19/Bi, 41/4.
SOUTH KINGSTON, R. I., 13/Bi.
SPAIN, 7/Bi.
SPANKTOWN, N. J. (CARTERET-RAHWAY, N. J.), 17/78.
SPARKS COLLECTION, CORNELL UNIVERSITY LIBRARY, 1, 3/1, 11/2, 11/5, 11/8, 11/12, 11/13, 11/19, 18/1, 18/3, 18/4, 18/5, 18/6, 18/7, 22/1, 29/1, 32/1, 34/1, 37/1, 51/B5, 51/B6, 51/B7, 51/B8, 51/E3.
SPARKS, JARED, 11/5, 11/19, 18/1, 34/1.
SPARKS MANUSCRIPTS, HARVARD UNIVERSITY LIBRARY, 14/last map, 51/A5, 51/A6, 51/B3, 51/B9, 51/B10, 51/C2, 51/C3, 51/D1, 51/E1.
SPENCER, GRIFFIN, 45/Bi.
SPENCER, GENERAL JOSEPH, 46/Bi.
SPRINGFIELD, MASS., 25/Bi.
SPRINGFIELD, N. J., 17/67B, 17/67C, 17/75, 17/75A, 17/75B, 17/107, 43/4B, 51/C2, 51/C3.
SQUIRE FULLERS, 14/117A.
STAFFORD COURT HOUSE, VA., 14/124N, 14/124O.
STAMFORD, CONN., 17/2nd unnumbered map, 17/24, 17/33, 17/34.
STANWICK, CONN., 17/24, 17/24-2nd.
STATEN ISLAND, N. Y., 3/Bi, 51/B12.
STEARNS, W. AND BIGELOW, D., 51/B11.
STEUBEN, BARON WILLIAM VON, 5/Bi.
STEVENS, HENRY N., 41/6.
STIRLING, LORD, see Alexander, William.
STONE, WILLIAM, 18/2.
STONINGTON, CONN., 13/Bi.
STONY POINT, N. Y. (STONE POINT, N. Y.), 18/Bi, 20/Bi, 37/Bi, 41/5, 47/5, 51/B6, 51/B8.
SUCCASUNNY, N. J., 4/1A, 4/1B, 14/117A.
SUFFOLK COUNTY COMPANY, 22/Bi.
SUFFRANS, N. Y.(SUFFERN, N. Y.), 17/C, 17/1, 17/42, 17/113, 17/113-2nd, 17/114, 50/1.
SULLIVAN, GENERAL JOHN, 1, 11/13, 17/Bi, 23/Bi, 27/103A, 42/Bi, 42/1, 46/Bi, 51/A6, 51/B2.
SUNBURY, PA., 27/103A-2nd route, 27/last map.
SUSQUEHANNA RIVER, 14/124D, 14/124E, 17/65, 17/95A, 17/95B, 17/95C, 17/95D, 17/95E, 17/95F, 17/95G, 17/95H, 17/95I, 17/95K, 21/52C-2nd piece, 23/9, 27/103A, 27/103B.
SUSSEX, N. J., 4/1B, 4/1C, 17/90C.
SUSSEX COURT HOUSE, N. J., 4/1, 14/119, 14/119A.
SUTTON, MASS., 37/Bi.
SWAN'S "BRITISH ARCHITECT", 33/Bi.
SWAN'S "COLLECTION OF DESIGNS IN ARCHITECTURE", 33/Bi.
SWEDE FORK ROAD, N. J., 17/73-1st, 17/73-2nd.

— T —

TALLMADGE, MAJOR BENJAMIN ("JOHN BOLTON", "S. G."), 51/BB, 51/BB7, 51/BB8, 51/BB9(?), 51/E2.
TANCKES, MATTHEW, 17/71C.